Indian chain stitch

MARIE PEACEY

δελος

CAPE TOWN

Dedicated to my husband, Basil and my daughters, Janeke, Annabeth and Carina. I would like to thank Annabeth for tracing my illustrations.

The three cushion covers on the front cover photograph were made by Jo Doyle.

The publishers would like to acknowledge:
Binnehuis Interiors, Cape Town
Brian Armino of Transoriental Carpet Co., Tyger Valley
Juliesen Framers, Stikland
Malabar Trading Company, Cape Town
Tradewinds, New Germany

© 1991 Delos, 40 Heerengracht, Cape Town

Also available in Afrikaans as **Indiese kettingsteek**

Cover design by Debbie Odendaal
Illustrations by Marie and Annabeth Peacey
Photography by André Stander
Photographs on cover (front) and pp. 9 and 12 by Anton de Beer
Typography by Robert B. Wouterse
Typeset in 10 on 12 pt Helvetica light
Printed and bound by Printkor, Cape Town
First edition, first impression 1991

ISBN 1-86826-192-1

Contents

Introduction

When trade links became more established between India, China and the western countries, more and more Western embroiderers found their inspiration in Eastern textiles and engravings from the days of Marco Polo.

The Indian subcontinent has a rich tradition of embroidery, with patterns and techniques varying from region to region. Beadwork, appliqué, mirror work and geometric patterns are all typically Indian. Free-style flower patterns, stylised figures, animals and birds, are also combined to make attractive borders and designs.

The district of Azerbaijan was once famous for its overlaid and inlaid appliqué. Pieces of woven wool or cotton fabric were held in place with parallel rows of tamboured chain stitch, embellished with local seed pearls or with gold and silver thread.

The Marsh Arabs, inhabitants of the South-East of Iraq, have a form of continuous chain stitch embroidery sometimes known as Kurdish work. Brightly-coloured wools almost completely cover a piece of loosely-woven fabric. The fabric is divided into various chain-stitched segments of motifs of camels, birds, or men on horseback. These segments are usually filled in with parallel lines of chain stitch. This embroidery is worked by men and made into rugs or wall-hangings which they sell. The older examples are mostly subdued in regard to colouring, while pieces worked recently tend to be almost garish, with bright pink and yellow predominating.

The Numdah or decorative rug from Kashmir is well known for its decorative chain stitch. This type of embroidery is worked either with a tambour hook or embroidery needle on a ground of matted felt, but sacking made from Bengali jute is also used.

The pattern is worked in crewel yarn or spinning yarn. The colours are limited, being subtle tones with one or two stronger hues to give contrast to the design. Even today

the colours remain traditionally muted and earthy. The general effect of the embroidery is harmonious and flowing, with no individual motif standing out from the others.

Men of Afghanistan do not normally have embroidered clothing, although in winter some of them wear sheepskin coats with decorations worked in brightly-coloured silk chain stitch. The skull caps worn by men, some women and boys, are made of cotton fabric with crowns cut in conical shapes. They are embroidered by men in buttonhole and chain stitch.

NUMDAH OR DECORATIVE RUG
The Numdah design can also be geometric with eight-pointed stars or similar motifs
(supplied by Transoriental Carpet Co.)

General instructions

Materials

Use any fabric like linen, cotton, synthetics or silk, but choose the most suitable fabric for your project according to its design and what it is going to be used for.

Embroidery needles have large eyes and come in various sizes. The larger the number of the needle, the finer and shorter it is. Choose the most suitable needle and thread for the fabric. If the needle is too large for the fabric and thread, it will leave holes in the fabric. Therefore you should test the needle and thread on the fabric to be used before starting. Keep the labels which have dye lot numbers with the thread until you have finished your project. Using an embroidery frame gives a neater appearance to the work.

Industrial yarns were used on most of the articles in this book. For very fine work topstitching cotton can be used. To create a varied texture, yarns of different thicknesses can be used on adjacent areas. Interesting effects can also be obtained by using various colours in the same thickness yarn or different thicknesses of yarn in the same colour.

A design can be outlined with thicker yarn and the areas in between filled with thinner yarn. Designs on printed material can be outlined or filled in to create texture or to accentuate certain colours. Curtain material decorated in this way can be used for making jackets. Thick wool can be embroidered on to jute or sacking to make a small carpet.

How to start

Leaving 5 cm of the thread on the wrong side (back), insert the needle from that side and bring it out on the right side (front). Insert the needle again at this starting point and bring it out a short distance further with the thread underneath the needle. This will form a loop and your first chain stitch (Fig. 1a).

Fig. 1a

How to finish off

Bring the thread through to the wrong side and weave 3 cm of the thread into the stitches before clipping it off (Fig. 1b).

Fig. 1b

How to join the thread

Join the old thread to the new thread with a knot on the wrong side. Start exactly where the previous stitch stopped (Fig. 2).

Fig. 2

Pressing and stretching

When stitches are worked very close together the fabric might pucker. Press on the wrong side with a steam iron to stretch evenly.

Stitches

Simple chain stitch

The simple chain stitch can be worked either with a needle or a tambour hook (a kind of crochet hook). It can be used as an outline and as a filler.

Simple chain stitch with a needle

Once the thread has been brought out at the required point, the needle is reinserted at the same point, leaving a small loop on the right side of the work; it is then brought out again at a point further along. This space determines the length of your stitch. The loop of thread is held with the thumb of the left hand and passed under the point of the needle. To make the next stitch, the needle is reinserted at the point where it was last drawn out, another loop is formed and the same process repeated (Fig. 3).

Fig. 3

Simple chain stitch with a tambour hook

The tambour stitch can be used as an embroidery stitch as seen on traditional Indian embroidery, and enriched with the addition of mirrors, or it can be used as a staying stitch using machine embroidery cotton worked in a zig-zag motion to secure heavier yarns in place. It can also be used to attach beads and sequins to the embroidery.

BLUE CUSHION COVER
This intricate design is simplified by using one colour in various shades for the embroidery (made by Elsie Smit)

This embroidery should be done on a frame with a stand, since both hands need to be free, one to hold the hook, and the other, the yarn (Fig. 4). The hook is used in the same way as the crochet hook, but the chain stitches are made through the fabric. Insert the hook into the fabric, with the thread held in the left hand under the work. It is then passed over the hook, and the hook is brought out again on the right side, the material being pressed downwards to prevent it from being pulled up by the hook which, as it returns, makes a chain stitch on the right side. Continue in this way, drawing the loop through the previous loop along the line of the design until it is finished (Fig. 5). Secure the starting point and ending of the work firmly so that the chain cannot pull out again.

The only difficulty with this kind of work is a tendency to confuse the movements of the hands. As long as you

Fig. 5

remember that the two actions of withdrawing the hook and pressing down the material must be performed simultaneously, it will be possible to produce a finished article in a comparatively short time. It is also advisable to use very tightly twisted thread, so that it cannot be split by the hook (cotton lace thread and pearl cotton).

Whipped chain stitch (Fig. 6)

Once the chain stitch is completed, each stitch is overcast with a thread of contrasting colour without penetrating the material beneath.

Fig. 4

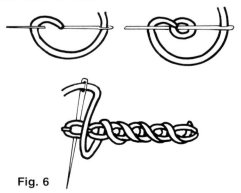

Fig. 6

7

BROWN CUSHION COVERS
These designs have made use of traditional motifs and colours with muted, subtle tones. One or two stronger hues give contrast to the designs (Cover, left, made by Rheta Grobler and cover, right, made by Brehette Agenbag)

Twisted chain stitch (Fig. 7)

This is the same as open chain with a twist at the top, and is a useful line stitch with a textured look. It is always worked downwards.

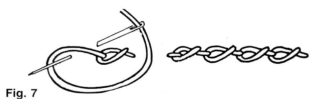

Fig. 7

Open chain (Fig. 8)

Made in the same way as the chain, except that the top of the loop is open; it could be worked closely together to make a solid line with little ground fabric showing through. This is the stitch most used on the antique wall-hanging shown on p. 13.

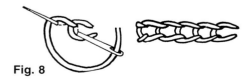

Fig. 8

Magic chain (Fig. 9)

Chain worked with two colours of thread in the same needle. Loop only the first colour under the needle for the first stitch. For the second stitch, loop the second colour under the needle. Alternate the colours in this way.

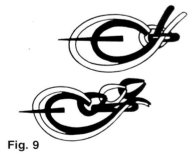

Fig. 9

Backstitched chain (Fig. 10)

After working a chain, backstitch through it as shown in the diagram.

Fig. 10

Zigzag chain stitch (Fig. 11)

Work as for ordinary chain stitch, slanting the stitches alternately to right and left.

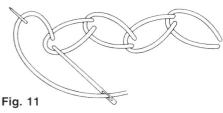

Fig. 11

Feathered chain stitch (Fig. 12)

This stitch is always worked downwards and consists of chain stitches worked to the left and right at a slant. It is essential that the stitches should be of an even size and equally spaced.

Fig. 12

Cable chain (Fig. 13)

This is worked the same way as a simple chain, but in this case the thread is twisted around the needle after each chain loop and before it enters the fabric, which makes a link between the chains.

Fig. 13

Broken chain (Fig. 14)

This is worked in the same way as the chain, inserting the needle outside the previous chain loop.

Fig. 14

BLACK CUSHION COVER
Bright colours used on a dark background enhance the symmetry of this design (made by Jo Doyle)

Detached chain or lazy daisy stitch (Fig. 15)

Instead of reinserting the needle inside the previous loop, make a tiny stitch over the loop to hold it in place. Work daisy stitches in the same way as for detached chain, but position the stitches to form a flower.

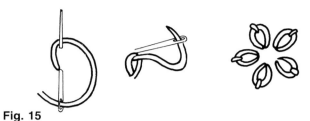

Fig. 15

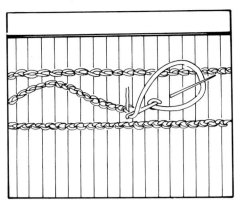

Fig. 16

Smocking in chain stitch (Fig. 16)

This design is worked entirely in chain stitch, and requires four rows of gathers about 1 cm apart.

Begin work at the top and to the left, with two horizontal rows of chain stitch. Next, work the loop design between these two rows. This consists of two waving lines of chain stitch, crossing each other at every seventh gather and forming regular ovals.

If it is used on clothing, buttons or a zip should be inserted as there is no stretch in this type of smocking.

Chain stitch as a filling stitch (Fig. 17)

It is always easier to work around shapes to keep the lines of the stitches close together. When working a design which is filled in with closely-packed stitches, choose a medium-weight fabric which is suitable for the weight of the stitching.

Work along all the lines of the design first to spread the tension evenly over the entire piece of embroidery.

Work the outline of the smaller shapes and then, as you return to the starting point, bring the needle point just

SMOCKED DRESS
Smocking in chain stitch was used on the front of this dress for a child (made by Ros Odendaal)

DETAIL OF NUMDAH
Note that the filling lines of chain stitch in the background are executed in circles and produce a design of their own (supplied by Transoriental Carpet Co.)

inside the first round of stitches so that the start of the second round is hardly visible. Continue like this until the background is completely filled in and the centre is reached. Bring the needle over the last loop and draw the yarn through to the back. Finish off.

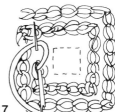

Fig. 17

Variations on chain stitch

The following stitches: open buttonhole stitch (Fig. 18), fly stitch (Fig. 19), feather stitch (Fig. 20) and lazy daisy stitch (Fig. 21), are all chain-related stitches. In each case the loop goes under the point of needle as seen in the chain stitch. The only difference is the place where the needle enters the fabric.

Fig. 18

Fig. 19

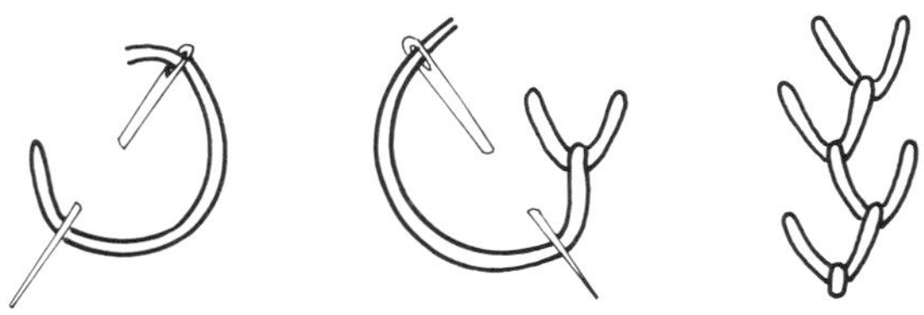

Fig. 20

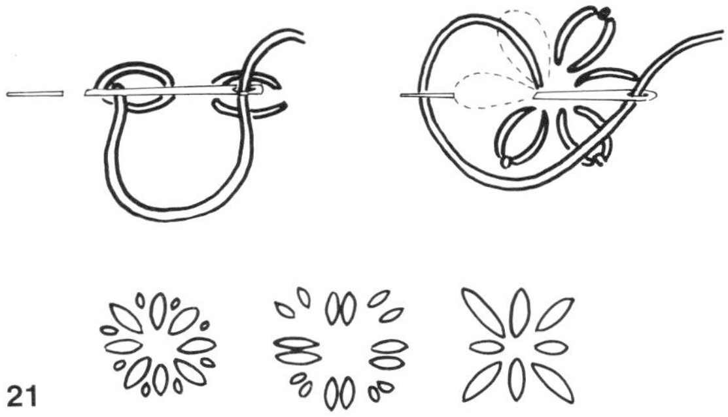

Fig. 21

TABLE CLOTH
By repeating smaller designs a larger, more intricate design can be achieved. The use of fewer colours prevents the design from being too overpowering (made by Jo Doyle)

Mirror work with sisha stitch (Fig. 22, a-f)

Mirror work is used for both clothing and decorative items. Small pieces of silvered glass or mica are attached to the ground fabric by a retaining network of stitches around their circumference.

Sisha stitch is a descriptive name for any of the stitches used for sewing down sisha glass. The older pieces of mirror work were done in more ethnic colours like rust, moss green and indigo, whereas today shocking pink and bright citron are combined on cushion covers, yokes, collars and cuffs of shirts or dresses, bags and belts.

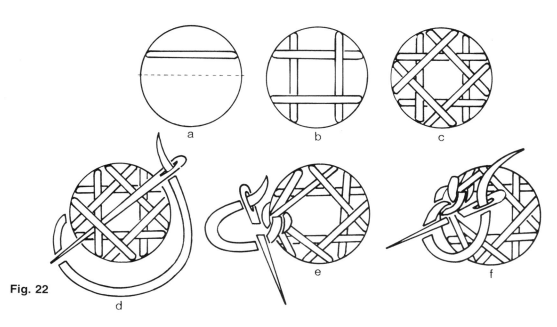

Fig. 22

ANTIQUE WALL-HANGING
This is an excellent example of mirror work with sisha stitch. Open chain stitch was mostly used on this piece (owned by Marie Peacey)

Spectacle case and purse

Spectacle case

Materials

Sturdy black material
Matching thread
Embroidery cotton
Embroidery needle
Dressmaker's carbon paper
Pins
Ballpoint pen
Foil (found as a sealer for some tins of instant coffees)
Fabric glue
Design (see p. 34)

Method

- Transfer the design on to the front and the flap of the spectacle case: place the dressmaker's carbon paper with the coloured side face down on the material. Put the design on top of the carbon and pin the design, carbon paper and material together. Trace the design on to the material with the ballpoint pen. Remove the design and carbon paper.
- Cut out small circles of foil and glue into position. Work sisha stitches over the edges.
- Embroider chain stitch on the rest of the design.
- Cut a lining for the spectacle case. Keeping the right sides together, stitch the side seams of the lining together.
- With the right sides together, stitch the side seams of the spectacle case together.
- With their wrong sides facing, place the lining inside the spectacle case and turn in the seam allowances around the edges of the case and lining around the opening and flap.
- Slipstitch the two pieces together.

SPECTACLE CASE AND PURSE
Chain stitch embroidery on thickly woven material with a design or printed material can add a textured look to the article. Certain colours can also be accentuated with slightly brighter thread, as seen on the purse made from a Dutch woven tablecloth (Spectacle case, centre back, made by Elsie Smit and purse, right, made by Marie Peacey)

Purse

Materials

Thickly woven material with
  design or printed material
Cotton material for lining
Matching thread
Bias binding
Zip
Press-stud
Embroidery cotton
Embroidery needle
Design (see p. 34)

Method

- Cut a rectangle measuring 16 cm x 12 cm out of printed or woven material.
- Cut the same shape out of cotton material for the lining.
- Tack the lining on top of material, with wrong sides facing.
- Divide the rectangle into three sections. Fold over an outer section on to the middle section.
- Fold raw edge under and tack one edge of the zip under the folded-in edge and stitch together. Do not stitch the zip to the bottom lining!
- Tack a piece of bias binding over the other side of the zip and stitch down on to the lining (Fig. 23).

Fig. 23

- Edge remaining raw edges of purse with bias binding. Sew on press-stud or fastener.
- Simply use the design woven into the material as a guide line. Choose complementary colours for the embroidery.

Painted tea-cosy

Materials for design

Javana silk paint
Pure cotton material
Matching thread
Embroidery cotton
Embroidery needle
Dish with clean water
Watercolour paintbrush
Hairdryer
Pencil
Design (see p. 35)

Method for design

- Prewash the cotton material for the design and dry it. It must be ironed smooth.

- Remember to work on a plastic-coated surface when using the paint. Paint circles or patterns on the fabric with various colours of your choice.

- Add more water with the paintbrush to allow the colours to flow into each other. Dry with a hairdryer.

- Place the painted material over the design and trace with a pencil along the lines, which will be clearly visible through the fabric.

- Cut out the various shapes and appliqué them on to the front of the tea-cosy.

If you do not wish to appliqué the design directly on to the tea-cosy, you could transfer it as follows: the front of the tea-cosy should be placed over the design against a window or a glass-topped table with light behind it. The lines will be visible through a light-coloured fabric even if it is thicker than a normal cotton material.

PAINTED TEA-COSY
Material which already has a printed design can be used as a guide for the embroidery. Pure cotton material can also be painted with Javana silk paints, as seen on this tea-cosy (made by Jeanne Stumpf)

Materials for tea-cosy

Material for tea-cosy
Material for lining
Matching thread
Batting
Bias binding

Method for tea-cosy

- Cut the pattern pieces out of material, batting and lining according to your own requirements.

- Appliqué the painted shapes on to the front of the tea-cosy.

- Decorate the front further with different chain stitches as seen on the tea-cosy in the photograph.

- With the right sides facing, tack the corded bias binding between the front and back of the tea-cosy. Keep the bottom edge open.

- Note that the raw edge of the bias binding must be on the same side as the raw edges of the front and back pieces.

- Stitch together around curve and turn inside out.

- With right sides facing, stitch the back and front of the lining together. Keep the bottom edge open.

- Place the batting inside the tea-cosy. Place the lining (with right sides facing) in the tea-cosy on top of the batting. Turn up the seam allowance around the bottom edges of the tea-cosy and the lining.

- Slipstitch the two pieces together.

Appliquéd shoulder bag

Materials

Denim material
Matching thread
Bias binding
Wool
Thick embroidery needle
Dressmaker's carbon
 paper
Ballpoint pen
Zip (optional)
Commercial woven strap
 for shoulder band (op-
 tional)
Design (see p. 35)

Method

- Cut the pattern pieces out of the denim material (Fig. 24).

- Transfer the design on to the front pattern piece: place the dressmaker's carbon paper with the coloured side face down on the material. Put the design on top of the carbon paper and trace it on to the material with a ballpoint pen.

- Appliqué bias binding on to the square, which is positioned diagonally across the bag, as well as around a circle of cotton material in the centre of the design (see photograph).

- Embroider parallel lines of chain stitch on the folded edges of the appliquéd work.

- Embroider chain stitch along the rest of the design lines.

- If the bag is to be made with a top gusset and zip, work as follows: stitch the zip into the top gusset. With right sides facing, stitch the short edges of either side gusset to the short edges of the base gusset. Stitch the short edges of the long gusset section (side/base/side) to the short edges of the top gusset. Open the zip and, still with right sides together, stitch the gussets to the front and back of the bag.

- If the bag is made without a gusset on top, work as follows: with right sides facing, stitch either side gusset to correspond with each short edge of the base gusset. Stitch the long gusset section (side/base/side) to the front and back of the bag.

- Overlock the raw edges of the seams and turn inside out.

- If you are using a commercial, woven strap for the band, measure distance from shoulder to position on hip where shoulder band will join the bag. Double the measurement.

- If you are going to make your own shoulder band out of denim material, measure distance from shoulder to position on hip where shoulder band will join the bag. Double the measurement and cut the band about 10 cm wide. With right sides facing, stitch the long sides and one short side together. Turn inside out. Sew remaining open side closed with small hem stitches. Stitch the ends of shoulder bands to the side gussets.

- The bias binding piping on the edges is optional, but gives the bag an attractive finished look.

SHOULDER BAGS
Although both bags are made in the same way, the designs on the front are worked differently (made by Marie Peacey)

	88 cm	
front	back
side	side
base	top (optional with zip)

70 cm

12 cm 12 cm 12 cm

44 cm

Fig. 24

Tea-cosy and toaster cover

Tea-cosy

Materials

Coarsely woven material
Matching thread
Tissue paper
Wool
Embroidery needle
Thin needle and thread
Material for lining
Batting
Bias binding
Design (see p. 36)

Method

- Cut pattern pieces out of woven material and lining.

- Transfer the design on to the front pattern piece of the tea-cosy, following the method using tissue paper as described for the wall-hanging with figures on p. 23.

- Outline the design with chain stitch and proceed to fill in the areas as seen on the example in the photograph.

- Complete the tea-cosy using the method described for the painted tea-cosy on p. 16.

TEA-COSY AND TOASTER COVER
The striped toaster cover clearly shows the effect of chain stitch embroidery along a design line. The tea-cosy, on the other hand, has a design which has been filled in with chain stitch (made by Marie Peacey)

Toaster cover

Materials

Sturdy striped cotton
  material for cover
Cotton material for lining
Matching thread
Bias binding
Industrial yarn
Thick embroidery needle
Dressmaker's carbon paper
Ballpoint pen
Design (see p. 36)

Method

- Cut the pattern pieces (back, front and gusset) out of the material and lining according to your own requirements.

- Transfer the design on to the front pattern piece: place the dressmaker's carbon paper with the coloured side face down on the material. Put the design on top of the carbon paper and trace it on to the material with a ballpoint pen.

- Using industrial yarn, embroider along the design line with chain stitch. Filling stitch and French knots were also used to complete the design.

- With right sides facing, tack the bias binding between the front and back pattern pieces and the gusset. Note that the raw edge of the bias binding must be on the same side as the raw edges of the front and back pieces.

- Stitch together along the seams, keeping the bottom edge open. Overlock the raw edges of the seams and turn inside out.

- With right sides facing, stitch the gusset between the front and back pattern pieces of the lining. Keep the bottom edge open.

- Place the lining (with right sides facing) inside the toaster cover. Turn up a small hem allowance along the bottom edge of the cover and lining. Slipstitch the two pieces together.

Striped shoulder bag

Materials

Denim material for bag
Striped cotton material for
  design backing
Matching thread
Dressmaker's carbon
  paper
Industrial yarn
Thick embroidery needle
Ballpoint pen
Zip (optional)
Commercial woven strap
  for shoulder band (op-
  tional)
Design (see p. 37)

Method

This bag is made in the same way as the previous bag (p. 18), but the design is worked in a different way.

- Cut a square out of striped material to fit the front of the bag.

- Transfer the design on to the front pattern piece: place the dressmaker's carbon paper with the coloured side face down on the material. Put the design on top of the carbon paper and trace it on to the material with a ballpoint pen.

- Outline the design with a single line of chain stitch in a contrasting colour or in the same colour as one of the stripes. To obtain a bolder effect, a double line of chain stitch can be worked along the design line.

- Tack the embroidered square on to the front of the bag. Fold the raw edges under and sew into position by hand, using small hem stitches, or by sewing machine.

- Complete shoulder bag using the method described for the appliquéd shoulder bag on p. 18.

Wall-hanging with figures

Materials

Coarsely woven material
Tissue paper
Thin needle and thread
Ballpoint pen
Wool
Thick embroidery needle
Design (see p. 38)

Method

- Transfer the motif on to the material with tissue paper: trace the design on to tissue paper. Pin the paper into position on the fabric. With small running stitches work along all the design lines. Pull the tissue paper off.

- Do not transfer every detail of the design, as embroidering without guidelines will add a pleasant and original quality to the work.

- Make a copy or photostat of the design and colour in some areas as a further guide.

- Begin by working all the marked outlines of the design in one colour.

- Fill in the segments with single lines and solid blocks of closely worked chain stitch, using the copy or photostat as a colour guide.

WALL-HANGING WITH FIGURES
The designs used in this piece are traditional and are typical of this type of work. Filling stitch has been used throughout to complete the designs (made by Christine Griffiths)

Wall-hanging with face

Materials

Coarsely woven cream
  material
Coarsely woven brown
  material
Matching thread
Tissue paper
Ballpoint pen
Thin needle and thread
Wool
Embroidery needle
Design (see p. 39)

Method

- Transfer the design on to the cream material with tissue paper: trace the design on to tissue paper. Pin the paper into position on the fabric. With small running stitches work along all the design lines. Pull the tissue paper off.

- Outline the design with chain stitch.

- Proceed to fill in the areas around the face with different chain stitches.

- Work satin stitch over the bottom part of the earring, leaving the ends loose to form a tassle.

- Secure the tassle with backstitch against the edge of the earring.

- Cut out the shape of the embroidered material, leaving 1 cm all around for hem allowance.

- Tack the embroidered piece of material in the centre of the brown material, and appliqué with small hem stitches.

- Fold the raw sides and bottom of the wall-hanging on to the wrong side.

- Fold again and stitch down.

- Fold the raw edge to the wrong side of the top edge and fold again to allow a rod to go through the opening and tack. Stitch down.

- Insert a rod and hang.

WALL-HANGING WITH FACE
**Coarsely woven material provides an ideal background for this bold, colourful design. A variety of chain stitches add texture to the design
(made by Marie Peacey)**

Cream cushion cover

Materials

Coarsely woven material (or calico)
Wool (or crochet yarn used for candlewicking)
Matching thread
Design (see p. 40)

Method

- Cut the square for the front piece of the cushion according to your own requirements.
- Cut two pieces to fit the front but large enough to overlap one another in the centre back by 20 cm.
- If you are using coarsely woven material, transfer the design according to the method described on p. 23. If you are using calico, transfer the design according to the method described on p. 16.
- Outline the design with chain stitch, using wool on coarsely woven material and crochet yarn on calico.
- Stitch a hem along both short sides of the overlapping pieces.
- With right sides facing, tack the two overlapping back pieces to the front of the cushion.
- Stitch the pieces together along their outer edges and turn inside out.
- Slip a cushion through the opening where the two back pieces overlap.

CREAM CUSHION COVER
By using material and wool of the same colour for this piece, a subtle effect is achieved (made by Marie Peacey)

Curtain tie-back

Materials

Material for tie-back
Matching thread
Bias binding
Embroidery needle
Industrial yarn
Button
Design (see p. 41)

Method (make 2)

- Cut two tie-backs out of the material, adapting the basic pattern on p.41 to suit your own requirements. One piece is used for the front, the other for the lining.

- Transfer the design on to the front pattern piece, using either the method described on p. 16 or the carbon paper method on p. 14.

- Outline the design with a darker colour, fill in the inner areas with a lighter colour.

- With wrong sides facing, tack the lining to the front piece.

- Stitch the two pieces together along the outer edges.

- Finish off the raw edges with bias binding. Sew on a button and loop as fastening.

CURTAIN TIE-BACK
A simple design completed with filling stitch can be very effective when two or more shades of the same colour are used. Bias binding finishes off the article neatly (made by Jeanne Stumpf)

Animals

Materials

Thin cotton material
Industrial yarn or embroi-
  dery cotton
Embroidery needle

Method

- Transfer the designs on to thin cotton material, using the method described on p. 16. Allow enough space between the various designs.

- Outline the designs first and then, using filling stitch, embroider them with colours of your own choice. As can be seen on the photograph, conventional colours need not be used, which add to the charm of the animals.

- Cut out the animal shapes, making an allowance of 5 cm all around.

- Fold the 5 cm edge under and appliqué the animals with small hem stitches on to bags, garments or a wall-hanging for a nursery.

ANIMALS
Simple designs can be transformed by using a range of colours. Filling stitch actually stiffens and supports the thinner sections of the designs (made by Zulu girls on the South Coast of Natal)

Table runner

Materials

Coarsely woven material
Matching thread
Lace for trimming
Industrial yarn
Embroidery needle
Tissue paper
Ballpoint pen
Design (see p. 42)

Design (see p. 42)

Method

• Cut a rectangle out of the material according to your requirements.

• Transfer the design on to the material as follows: trace the design on to tissue paper. Pin the paper into position on the fabric. With small running stitches work along all the design lines. Pull the tissue paper off.

• Using colours of your choice, embroider the design with chain stitch. Some or all of the design areas can be completed using filling stitch (see photograph).

• Fold under a hem allowance of 1 cm along the edges to the back. Sew by hand using small hem stitches or stitch with a sewing machine.

• Sew the lace trimming on to the short edges of the table runner.

TABLE RUNNER
Designs and colours can be selected to match your favourite dinner service and table cloth (made by Lyda van Wezel)

Tray cloth and napkin

Materials

Finely woven material
Matching thread
Lace for trimming
Embroidery cotton
Embroidery needle
Dressmaker's carbon
  paper
Ballpoint pen
Design (see p. 41)

Method

- Cut pattern pieces for the tray cloth and matching napkin(s) according to your requirements.

- Transfer the design on to the material as follows: place the dressmaker's carbon paper with the coloured side face down on the material. Put the design on top of the carbon paper and trace it on to the material with a ballpoint pen. You could also use the method described on p. 16 to transfer the design, provided your material has a light colour.

- Outline the design with chain stitch and use filling stitch to complete it.

- Fold under a small hem allowance along the edges to the back. Tack into position.

- Sew the lace trimming along the edges either by hand or sewing machine. You will automatically stitch down the hem as well.

TRAY CLOTH AND NAPKIN
The pattern in the material is enhanced by the embroidered design. Embroidery cotton gives the design a very glossy look (made by Jeanne Stumpf)

Designs

Design detail on rug (title page)

Design detail on rug (title page)

Design detail on rug (p. 5)

Design detail on rug (p. 5)

Spectacle case (p. 14)

Purse (p. 15)

34

Painted tea-cosy (p. 16)

Appliquéd shoulder bag (p.18)

Tea-cosy (p. 20)

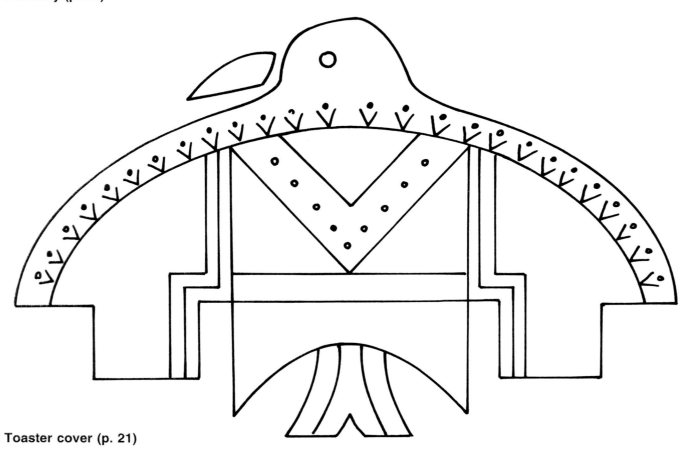

Toaster cover (p. 21)

36

Striped shoulder bag (p. 22)

Wall-hanging with figures (p. 23)

38

Wall-hanging with face (p. 24)

Cream cushion cover (p. 25)

fold

Curtain tie-back (p. 26)

Tray cloth and napkin (p. 29)

Table runner (p. 28)

42

Blue cushion cover (p. 7)

Brown cushion cover (p. 8, left)

Brown cushion cover (p. 8, right)

Table cloth (p. 12)

Pink, orange and blue cushion cover (on front cover)

GREEN BOND MARKET SURVEY FOR MALAYSIA

INSIGHTS ON THE PERSPECTIVES OF
INSTITUTIONAL INVESTORS AND UNDERWRITERS

NOVEMBER 2022

ASIAN DEVELOPMENT BANK

CONTENTS

TABLE, FIGURES, AND BOXES

ACKNOWLEDGMENTS

The lead authors—Kosintr Puongsophol, Oth Marulou Gagni, and Alita Lestor—all from the Economic Research and Regional Cooperation Department of the Asian Development Bank, would like to particularly thank Satoru Yamadera, Richard Supangan, Shu Tian, Roselyn Regalado, and Russ Jason N. Lo, all from Economic Research and Regional Cooperation Department, for their support and contributions. Editing by Kevin Donahue. Design and layout by Prince Nicdao.

The lead authors would like to thank the Global Green Growth Institute team—comprising Srinath Komarina, Hien Tran, Thinh Tran, Minh Tran, and Ha Nguyen—for their inputs and suggestions.

Finally, we would like to express our heartfelt gratitude to the Malaysian regulatory authorities and industry associations, as well as to all respondents, for their assistance with and participation in the survey. Local regulatory authorities include the Bank Negara Malaysia and Securities Commission Malaysia. Furthermore, we would like to thank RAM Sustainability, the National Mortgage Corporation of Malaysia, and the Federation of Investment Managers Malaysia for their support and sharing their inputs.

ABBREVIATIONS

ABMI	ASEAN+3 Asian Bond Markets Initiative
ADB	Asian Development Bank
ASEAN	Association of Southeast Asian Nations
ASEAN+3	ASEAN plus the People's Republic of China, Japan, and the Republic of Korea
BNM	Bank Negara Malaysia
EPF	Employees Provident Fund
ESG	environmental, social, and governance
ICM	Capital Markets Malaysia
JC3	Joint Committee on Climate Change
LCY	local currency
NGFS	Network of Central Banks and Supervisors for Greening the Financial System
SCM	Securities Commission Malaysia
SRI	Sustainable and Responsible Investment (Sukuk Framework)
TA	technical assistance
USD	United States dollar

SUMMARY AND KEY FINDINGS

SURVEY HIGHLIGHTS

▶ The online survey was conducted in January–February 2022 and received a total of 65 responses from 59 institutional investors representing the demand side and 6 financial advisors and underwriters representing the supply side. Institutional investors include 9 asset management companies, 1 development financial institution, 1 hedge fund, 33 insurance companies, 2 investment banks, 12 commercial banks, and 1 state-owned bank.

▶ While all investor and underwriter respondents expressed interest in either investing in or underwriting green bonds, some may be more prepared to do so than others. This is an area where development partners can potentially assist interested entities with technical assistance and capacity building.

▶ Renewable energy, energy efficiency, water management, and waste management are viewed as the most promising sectors for growth in Malaysia's green bond market.

▶ While there is a strong preference for small ticket sizes (less than USD10 million) from investors' point of view, underwriters and advisors are hoping for much bigger deals (more than USD50 million).

▶ The lack of a pipeline for eligible projects and an insufficient supply of green bonds are the two biggest barriers to the growth of the green bond market in Malaysia, according to both investors and underwriters.

▶ Most investors said that more policy guidance and clarity from regulators is needed to support the growth of Malaysia's green bond market, while underwriters said that a larger pipeline of green projects is the most important factor in spurring more issuances.

M alaysia's green bond market has enormous potential for growth. The majority of institutional investors who took part in the survey said they were creating action plans to include environmental, social, and governance (ESG) pillars in their investment strategies, and half of the underwriters who responded said they were creating plans to encourage clients to issue more green bonds. While investors and underwriters are both making the necessary preparations to expand their green bond portfolios, 14% of institutional investors do not yet have any exposure to green investments, and 17% of underwriters reported that their clients are not currently interested in the issuance of green bonds.

Renewable energy, energy efficiency, water management, and waste management are the sectors with the highest growth potential. Institutional investors and underwriters who represent both the supply and demand sides of the question agreed that renewable energy, energy efficiency, water management, and waste management have the greatest growth potential (**Table**). In fact, the majority of investor portfolios in the Malaysian green bond market already consist of investments in these sectors.

Table: Sectors with the Most Potential for Green Bond Issuances and Investments (%)

Investors			Underwriters			
Renewable Energy	Energy Efficiency	Water Management	Renewable Energy	Energy Efficiency	Water Management	Waste Management
29	19	16	23	19	14	14

Source: Survey details.

Unlike underwriters, investors have a strong preference for smaller issuance amounts. Nearly 41% of investors are looking for investment transactions totaling less than USD10 million, and 36% are interested in transactions with investments of up to USD50 million. In contrast, almost 33% of underwriters prefer issuance sizes of between USD11 million and USD50 million, while another 33% prefer issuance sizes of more than USD100 million. The majority of investors have stated that when making investment decisions, they give the most significant weight to credit rating, potential ESG impacts, and the company profile.

Demand from investors is extremely important. Underwriters believe that increased demand from investors is crucial to driving more issuance of green bonds and to encouraging potential issuers to integrate ESG considerations into their operations. In fact, preferential buying by public pension funds and central banks would demonstrate leading by example. Underwriters also believe that tax incentives and/or subsidies for issuers are equally important.

An insufficient supply of green bonds and the lack of a green project pipeline are the two most critical obstacles to the market's development. Institutional investors and underwriters emphasized two main barriers preventing Malaysia's green bond market from growing. The most important factor from the perspective of investors is the scarcity of green bonds. The majority of underwriters stated that the main obstacle preventing their clients from issuing green bonds is the lack of a pipeline of green projects. Another major barrier cited by both investors and underwriters is the lack of obvious advantages to investing in and issuing green bonds, which was followed by a lack of knowledge and resources. Investors have consequently suggested that clear government guidance and definitions of what constitutes "green" could facilitate greater issuance, while underwriters concurred that the most important policy option is to increase the pipeline of green projects.

INTRODUCTION

Background and Objective

The Asian Development Bank (ADB) is collaborating closely with the Association of Southeast Asian Nations (ASEAN), the People's Republic of China, Japan, and the Republic of Korea—collectively known as ASEAN+3—to promote the development of local currency (LCY) bond markets and regional bond market integration through the Asian Bond Markets Initiative (ABMI). The ABMI was established in 2002 to bolster the resilience of ASEAN+3 financial systems by developing LCY bond markets as an alternative source to foreign-currency-denominated, short-term bank loans for long-term investment financing.

ADB, as Secretariat for the ABMI, is implementing a regional technical assistance program to promote sustainable LCY bond market development with support from the People's Republic of China Poverty Reduction and Regional Cooperation Fund. This technical assistance was developed and is being implemented with guidance from ASEAN+3 finance ministers and central bank governors, and in accordance with the ABMI Medium-Term Road Map for 2019–2022.

This survey report, conducted in collaboration with the Global Green Growth Institute, aims to assess institutional investors' interest in green bonds issued in Malaysia, as well as the perspectives of local arrangers and underwriters on their clients' interest in green bond issuance. The survey aims to identify market drivers, impediments, and development priorities for Malaysia's sustainable finance market to assist development partners in identifying potential areas of support to accelerate the development of Malaysia's sustainable finance market.

Methodologies

ADB and the GGGI conducted the survey via an online platform in January–February 2022 and received a total of 65 responses from 59 institutional investors representing the demand side and 6 financial advisors and underwriters representing the supply side. Institutional investors included 9 asset management companies, 1 development financial institution, 1 hedge fund, 33 insurance companies, 2 investment bank, 12 commercial banks, and 1 state-owned bank.

OVERVIEW OF MALAYSIA'S SUSTAINABLE BOND MARKET

The Sustainable and Responsible Investment (SRI) Sukuk Framework, introduced by the Securities Commission Malaysia (SCM) in 2014 to facilitate the financing of sustainable and responsible investment initiatives, marked the start of Malaysia's sustainable finance market. Since then, the sustainable finance market has developed rapidly due to the joint efforts of relevant regulators and industry players.

As co-chair of the Association of Southeast Asian Nations (ASEAN) Capital Markets Forum's Sustainable Finance Working Group, the SCM is playing a critical role in the development of the ASEAN Green, Social, and Sustainability Bond Standards. In fact, after the ASEAN Green Bond Standards (AGBS) were launched in Malaysia in 2017, the first green bond issued under the AGBS was a *sukuk* (Islamic bond) issued by a Malaysian entity in the same year.

The total outstanding amount of green, social, and sustainability bonds in Malaysia was approximately USD6.1 billion at the end of June 2022, with private sector issuances leading the way (**Figure 1**).

The green bond market in Malaysia grew significantly following the announcement of the AGBS in 2017. This trend continued when the ASEAN Social Bond and Sustainability

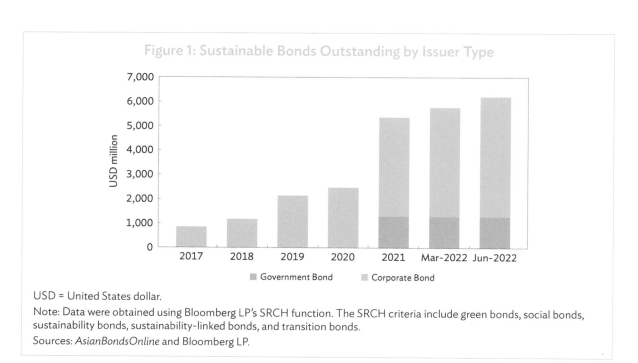

Figure 1: Sustainable Bonds Outstanding by Issuer Type

USD = United States dollar.
Note: Data were obtained using Bloomberg LP's SRCH function. The SRCH criteria include green bonds, social bonds, sustainability bonds, sustainability-linked bonds, and transition bonds.
Sources: *AsianBondsOnline* and Bloomberg LP.

Bond Standards were launched in 2018. In 2021, sustainable bond issuance expanded significantly, led by the Government of Malaysia's USD1.3 billion Sustainability Sukuk issuance, which was oversubscribed by 6.4 times (**Figure 2**). Malaysia's maiden Sustainability Sukuk issuance was the world's first USD-denominated sustainability *sukuk* issued by a sovereign, with proceeds going to eligible social and green projects aligned with the United Nations' Sustainable Development Goals.[1]

Relative to the green and sustainability bond market, the social bond market in Malaysia is relatively insignificant. The *sukuk* issued in 2015 and 2017 by Khazanah Nasional Berhad, Malaysia's sovereign wealth fund, under the SRI Sukuk Framework were considered social *sukuk* as the use of proceeds were for educational purposes. A majority of Malaysian issuers prefer the sustainability label for their bonds and *sukuk* because this gives the issuer greater flexibility regarding the use of proceeds.

According to the *Sustainability Bond Guidelines* published by the International Capital Market Association, sustainability bonds are bonds in which the proceeds are exclusively applied to finance or refinance green and/or social projects. Certain social projects may also have environmental co-benefits, and certain green projects may have social co-benefits. The classification of a use-of-proceeds bond as either a green, social, or sustainability bond should be determined by the issuer based on the primary objectives of the underlying projects. For example, a sustainability bond can be used to finance or refinance the development of energy-efficient affordable housing projects, such as the sustainability bond issued by Thailand's National Housing Authority.[2]

In terms of the currency, most sustainable bonds outstanding from Malaysian issuers at the end of the second quarter of 2022 were denominated in ringgit. Slightly more than 40%

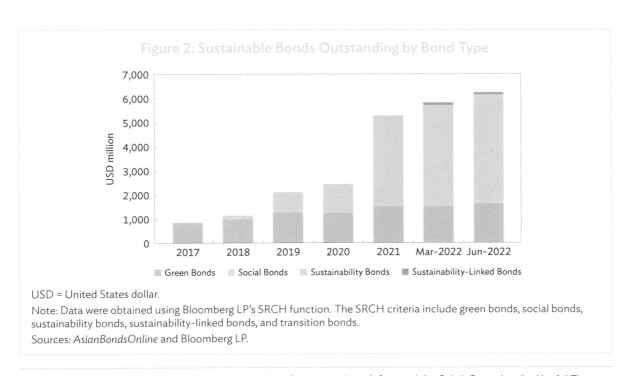

Figure 2: Sustainable Bonds Outstanding by Bond Type

USD = United States dollar.
Note: Data were obtained using Bloomberg LP's SRCH function. The SRCH criteria include green bonds, social bonds, sustainability bonds, sustainability-linked bonds, and transition bonds.
Sources: *AsianBondsOnline* and Bloomberg LP.

[1] Government of Malaysia, Ministry of Finance. 2021. *Press Citations*. Malaysia's Sustainability Sukuk Oversubscribed by 6.4 Times. 22 April.
[2] Government of Malaysia, National Housing Authority. 2021. *Sustainable Finance Framework*. Putrajaya.

of sustainable bonds and *sukuk* were issued in a foreign currency, with the majority of these denominated in United States (US) dollars, including the Government of Malaysia's maiden sustainability *sukuk* (**Figure 3**).

Financial institutions in Malaysia are the largest issuers of sustainable bonds, followed by the government and the real estate sector (**Figure 4**). As one of the pioneering regulatory leaders in Southeast Asia in pursuit of a standardized classification system for climate-related exposures, the Bank Negara Malaysia encouraged financial institutions to issue sustainable bonds with the release of the *Climate Change and Principle-based Taxonomy* in April 2021.[3]

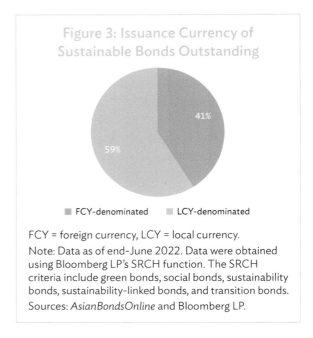

Figure 3: Issuance Currency of Sustainable Bonds Outstanding

■ FCY-denominated   ■ LCY-denominated

FCY = foreign currency, LCY = local currency.
Note: Data as of end-June 2022. Data were obtained using Bloomberg LP's SRCH function. The SRCH criteria include green bonds, social bonds, sustainability bonds, sustainability-linked bonds, and transition bonds.
Sources: *AsianBondsOnline* and Bloomberg LP.

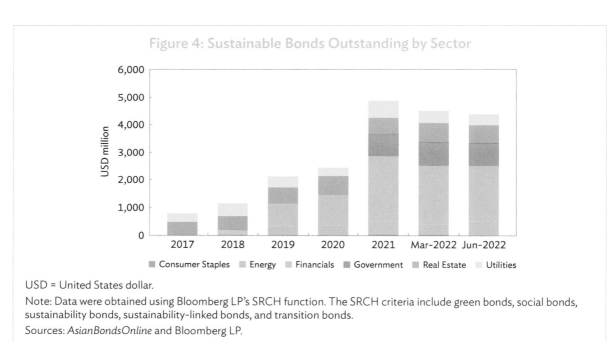

Figure 4: Sustainable Bonds Outstanding by Sector

■ Consumer Staples   ■ Energy   ■ Financials   ■ Government   ■ Real Estate   ■ Utilities

USD = United States dollar.
Note: Data were obtained using Bloomberg LP's SRCH function. The SRCH criteria include green bonds, social bonds, sustainability bonds, sustainability-linked bonds, and transition bonds.
Sources: *AsianBondsOnline* and Bloomberg LP.

---

[3]   Bank Negara Malaysia. 2021. *Climate Change and Principle-based Taxonomy*. Kuala Lumpur.

Despite its rapid expansion in 2021, the LCY corporate sustainable bond market remains small in comparison to the country's overall LCY corporate bond market (**Figure 5**). LCY sustainable bonds from corporate issuers accounted for only about 2% of LCY corporate bonds outstanding at the end of June 2022. However, this share has rapidly increased from a very low base, demonstrating the opportunity to promote more issuances of LCY sustainable bonds in Malaysia, especially from corporate issuers.

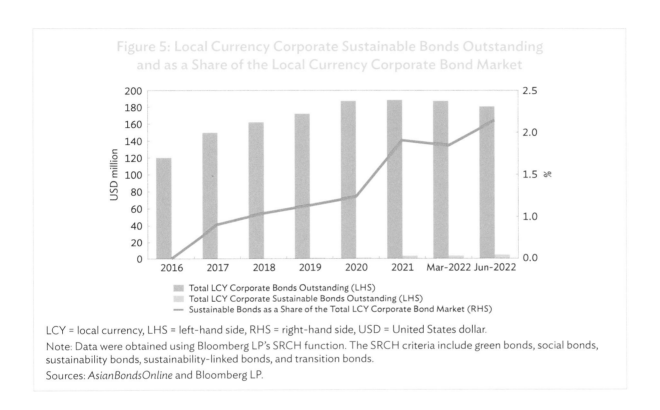

Figure 5: Local Currency Corporate Sustainable Bonds Outstanding and as a Share of the Local Currency Corporate Bond Market

- ▮ Total LCY Corporate Bonds Outstanding (LHS)
- ▮ Total LCY Corporate Sustainable Bonds Outstanding (LHS)
- — Sustainable Bonds as a Share of the Total LCY Corporate Bond Market (RHS)

LCY = local currency, LHS = left-hand side, RHS = right-hand side, USD = United States dollar.

Note: Data were obtained using Bloomberg LP's SRCH function. The SRCH criteria include green bonds, social bonds, sustainability bonds, sustainability-linked bonds, and transition bonds.

Sources: *AsianBondsOnline* and Bloomberg LP.

RECENT INITIATIVES IN SUSTAINABLE FINANCE

SRI initiatives began in 2014 when the Securities Commission Malaysia (SCM) introduced the SRI Sukuk Framework to facilitate the financing of sustainable and responsible investment initiatives. The launch of the SRI Sukuk Framework in 2014 signaled the initiation of the SCM's sustainable and responsible investment initiatives in line with its existing Capital Market Masterplan 2 to promote socially responsible financing and investment.[4]

Development of the sustainable finance market in Malaysia is being undertaken through a coordinated approach led by the Joint Committee on Climate Change (JC3). The JC3, co-chaired by the BNM and the SCM, was established in 2019 and comprises senior officials from Bursa Malaysia and 21 industry players.[5] The JC3 is guided by three key mandates:

(i) building capacity through the sharing of knowledge, expertise, and best practices in assessing and managing climate-related risks;

(ii) identifying issues, challenges, and priorities facing the financial sector in managing the transition toward a low-carbon economy; and

(iii) facilitating collaboration between stakeholders in advancing coordinated solutions to address emerging challenges and issues.

Following the JC3's inaugural meeting in September 2019, subcommittees were formed covering the following areas: (i) risk management, (ii) governance and disclosure, (iii) products and innovation, and (iv) engagement and capacity building. In 2021, another subcommittee on bridging data gaps was established to identify crucial data and relevant data sources and to explore potential solutions to minimize data gaps for the purpose of managing climate- and environment-related risks within the financial sector and of strengthening the structure of green finance solutions.[6]

In March 2022, the JC3 released for public consultation the draft Task Force on Climate-related Financial Disclosures' Application Guide for Malaysian Financial Institutions to provide key recommendations and assist financial institutions in preparing for climate-related disclosures. This followed the earlier announcement that financial institutions would be required to make mandatory climate-related financial risk disclosures aligned with the Task Force on Climate-related Financial

---

[4] SC. 2014. *Media Release*. SC Introduces Sustainable and Responsible Investment Sukuk Framework. 28 August.

[5] BNM and SC. 2022. *News Release*. Accelerating the Financial Sector's Response to Climate Risk. 27 April.

[6] BNM. 2019. *News Release*. Inaugural Meeting of Joint Committee on Climate Change. 27 September.

Disclosures beginning in 2024.[7] In addition, the JC3 plans to develop a climate disclosure guide for Malaysian companies. This guide aims to improve the quality and accessibility of information on business resilience to climate-related risks. This would encourage financial flows to climate mitigation and adaptation actions, including among small and medium-sized businesses. JC3 members also agreed to identify cross-cutting and strategic issues arising from the International Sustainability Standards Board's draft Sustainability Disclosure Standards and to consider providing a collective response, especially from the perspective of a developing economy.[8]

In April 2022, the JC3 also released a *Report on the Sustainable Finance Landscape in Malaysia* to understand and assess the current state of sustainability practices and readiness within the financial sector. The survey was conducted in November 2021 and focuses on four key aspects of sustainability practices:[9]

(i)   sustainability commitment and strategy,
(ii) governance and risk management,
(iii) green products and solutions, and
(iv) climate disclosure.

The year 2021 was also significant for the development of sustainable finance in Malaysia with the issuance of sustainability *sukuk* by the Government of Malaysia. The *sukuk* were offered via two tranches: USD800 million of 10-year trust certificates and USD500 million of 30-year trust certificates. The *sukuk* were so well received by investors that the government decided to

increase the issuance size from USD1.0 billion to USD1.3 billion. This *sukuk* issuance was unique because its underlying assets are sustainable, consisting of travel vouchers for Malaysia's Light Rail Transit, Mass Rapid Transit, and KL Monorail networks.[10]

The BNM was among the first central banks in ASEAN to release the *Climate Change and Principle-based Taxonomy* for financial institutions in April 2021. The taxonomy (i) assists financial institutions in assessing and categorizing economic activities that meet climate objectives and promote transition to a low-carbon economy, and (ii) facilitates standardized classification and reporting of climate-related exposures to support risk assessments at the transactional and institutional levels.[11]

As an active member of the Network of Central Banks and Supervisors for Greening the Financial System's (NGFS) Steering Committee, the BNM pledged its support to the NGFS Glasgow Declaration for COP26.[12] The BNM also committed to undertake the six NGFS recommendations published in *A Call for Action: Climate Change as a Source of Financial Risk.*[13]

The SCM announced the expansion of the Green SRI Sukuk Grant Scheme in January 2021 to encourage more companies to finance green, social, and sustainability projects through SRI *sukuk* and bond issuance. The new grant scheme, known as the SRI Sukuk and Bond Grant Scheme, will be applicable to all *sukuk* issued under the SRI Sukuk Framework and

[7]   BNM and SC. 2021. *News Release.* Advancing the Financial Sector's Response to Climate Risk. 10 December.
[8]   Footnote 5.
[9]   JC3. 2022. *Report on the Sustainable Finance Landscape in Malaysia.*
[10] Footnote 1.
[11] BNM. 2021. *Climate Change and Principle-based Taxonomy.*
[12] BNM. COP26 Pledge: Our Commitment to Greening the Financial Sector.
[13] NGFS. 2019. *A Call for Action: Climate Change as a Source of Financial Risk.*

bonds issued under the ASEAN Green, Social, and Sustainability Bond Standards. Under the new scheme administered by Capital Markets Malaysia (ICM), an affiliate of the SCM, eligible issuers can claim the grant to offset up to 90% of the external review costs incurred, subject to a maximum of MYR300,000 per issuance. Furthermore, income tax exemptions are provided for issuers who received support from the SRI Sukuk and Bond Grant Scheme for a period of 5 years (until 2025) as announced in Budget 2021.[14]

In September 2021, the SCM launched the third Capital Market Masterplan, which will serve as a strategic framework for the growth of Malaysia's capital market over the next 5 years. Among the six key development and regulatory thrusts, the third Capital Market Masterplan focuses on long-term value creation by (i) promoting responsible businesses with good corporate governance and (ii) facilitating the intermediation of capital to sustainable and responsible businesses through the SRI Sukuk Framework and ICM to cater to needs of the Malaysian economy. Strategic initiatives under the masterplan to promote sustainable finance include the following:[15]

Mobilizing Capital toward Sustainable and Responsible Businesses

(a) explore approaches for transition financing in Malaysia;
(b) facilitate wider options across the funding escalator for companies embarking on net-zero commitments;
(c) promote greater transparency in the market through disclosures; and
(d) evaluate approaches for investor protection in relation to the

management of disclosures, data, ESG investment decision-making, and greenwashing risks.

Expanding the Reach of ICM to the Broader Stakeholders of the Economy

(a) enable greater access to Sharia-compliant fundraising for micro, small, and medium-sized enterprises, focusing on those in the halal economy;
(b) develop guidance to facilitate the assessment of unlisted companies for Islamic fundraising activities;
(c) develop guidance to incorporate Sharia requirements and ESG best practices for public limited companies; and
(d) leverage and strengthen relevant ICM frameworks to enhance the Islamic social finance ecosystem.

Embracing Collaboration and Innovation for Growth

(a) position Malaysia as a hub for SRI by developing thought leadership, catering to regional capacity-building needs as well as championing innovation and research;
(b) enhance ICM global thought leadership to promote greater alignment of capital market activities with *maqasid al-Sharia* (objectives of Sharia);
(c) build capacity for ICM by strengthening the capabilities of practitioners in the area of Sharia governance and by developing talents for Islamic wealth management; and
(d) facilitate innovation in Islamic fintech through regulatory guidance and accelerator programs.

---

[14]   SC. 2021. *Media Release*. SRI Sukuk and Bond Grant Scheme to Encourage Capital Market Fund Raising for Sustainable Development. 21 January.

[15]   SC. Capital Market Masterplan 3.

In 2020, the first green bond verifier in Malaysia, RAM Sustainability, was accredited by the Climate Bonds Initiative.[16] Having a local green bond verifier with a good understanding of the local market environment and practices is an important factor in the sustainable finance ecosystem. The ESG service offerings provided by RAM Sustainability include second-party opinions on issuers' sustainability frameworks and ESG ratings for corporates and issuers (**Box 1**).

Box 1: RAM Sustainability—Supporting Climate Integrity in the Green Bond Market through Climate Bonds Standard Verification

RAM Sustainability, a wholly owned subsidiary of Malaysia's RAM Holdings Berhad (the group), commenced its sustainability services in 2016 offering second-party opinions, as well as sustainability ratings and environmental, social, and governance analytics for the financial market, leveraging the group's more than 30 years of experience in providing independent credit rating services, economic research and consultancy, and data analytics.

Since the launch of the Sustainable and Responsible Investment Sukuk Framework in 2014 and the Association of Southeast Asian Nations (ASEAN) Green, Social, and Sustainable Bond Standards in 2018, there has been increasing interest in the issuance of sustainable bonds and *sukuk* (Islamic bonds) in the domestic market. While these framework and standards provide guidance on the broad categories of eligible green projects, there is a need to further define the eligibility of green projects and their climate alignment as the market develops.

To support market needs and green finance market development in Malaysia, RAM Sustainability became an approved *Climate Bonds Standard and Certification Scheme* verifier in 2020. RAM Sustainability's application to become an approved verifier was primarily motivated by its goal to improve access to sustainable finance for ASEAN issuers by helping them demonstrate to the market that their green bonds, *sukuk,* and loans meet global best practice standards for climate integrity, management of proceeds, and transparency.

RAM Sustainability worked closely with the Asian Development Bank to deliver its climate bond verification service as part of the bank's developmental role in improving the sustainable finance ecosystem. RAM Sustainability is currently able to provide verification for up to seven out of the 15 sectors available for certification under the Climate Bonds Standard, including renewables, low-carbon transport, and low-carbon buildings, among others. The verifiable sectors are based on RAM Sustainability's experience in providing second-opinion and sustainability services in the relevant sectors.

Source: RAM Sustainability.

---

[16] RAM Sustainability. 2020. RAM Sustainability's Climate Bonds Approved Verifier Status Strengthens Malaysia's Position as Sustainable Finance Centre. Press release. 18 August.

SURVEY RESULTS

The survey was conducted in January–February 2022 among local institutional investors—including fund managers, financial institutions, and insurance companies—as well as local underwriters and advisors. A summary of the survey's findings is given below.

Institutional Investors

The survey began by asking respondents about their firms' interest and/or current investment in green bonds. The majority of respondents indicated there was interest in green bonds and that their respective firms are currently developing an action plan, while others were exploring this field but with limited awareness and resources (**Figure 6**). None of the respondents indicated a lack of interest in green bonds. One asset management company reported having launched two SRI equity funds at the end of 2021 with plans to launch more sustainability-focused funds to cater to investors' preference for these products. Further, four insurance companies expressed a strong interest in green bonds, with one having already established a green investment mandate.

Almost 80% of respondents are still exploring and developing an action plan, with green bonds representing less than 5% of investor portfolios on average. Only two respondents, an asset management firm and an insurance company,

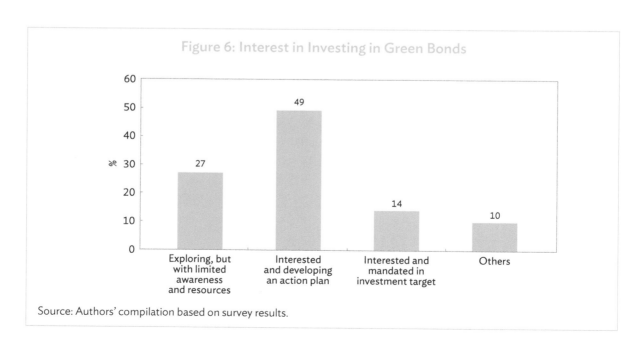

Figure 6: Interest in Investing in Green Bonds

Source: Authors' compilation based on survey results.

reported that green investments made up between 11% and 20% of their portfolios, while one insurance company reported that green investments made up between 21% and 30 % of its portfolio (**Figure 7**).

When asked about ticket size, 41% of respondents indicated a preference for investments of less than USD10 million, while 36% indicated a willingness to invest up to USD50 million per transaction (**Figure 8**).

Meanwhile, around 13% of respondents indicated that investment size depends on the credit profile, investment type, credit quality, and issue size of the bond.

Renewable energy (35%), water management (16%), and energy efficiency (12%) are the top sectors in terms of comprising a share of respondents' investment portfolios, while only 8% of respondents have invested in green bonds issued to finance green buildings (**Figure 9**).

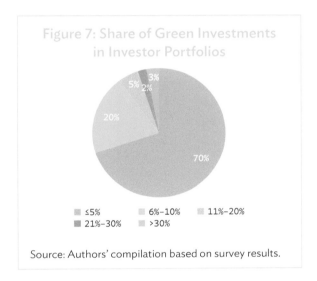

Figure 7: Share of Green Investments in Investor Portfolios

■ ≤5% ■ 6%–10% ■ 11%–20%
■ 21%–30% ■ >30%

Source: Authors' compilation based on survey results.

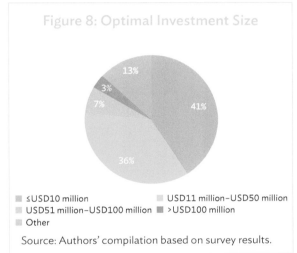

Figure 8: Optimal Investment Size

■ ≤USD10 million ■ USD11 million–USD50 million
■ USD51 million–USD100 million ■ >USD100 million
■ Other

Source: Authors' compilation based on survey results.

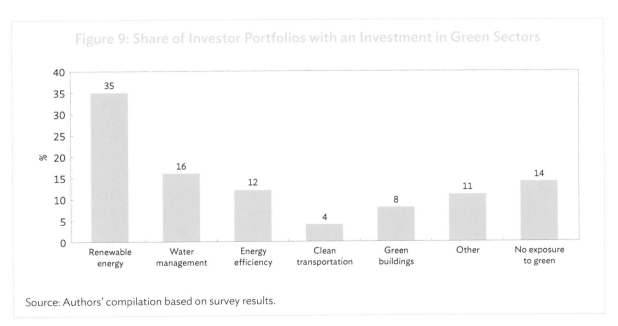

Figure 9: Share of Investor Portfolios with an Investment in Green Sectors

Source: Authors' compilation based on survey results.

While 14% of respondents have no exposure to green investments, this clearly indicates that the green bond and *sukuk* market in Malaysia has significant potential to expand further. While none of the respondents stated they had zero interest in investing in green bonds, there is still a need for local institutional investors to build their capacity and develop an action plan for making ESG investments. This can be an area where development partners collaborate with local regulators and industry associations to carry out more capacity-building programs for domestic capital market stakeholders, particularly local institutional investors.

The majority of investors believe that having a Sustainable Development Goals mandate in their institution's investment strategy is essential to investing in green bonds (**Figure 10**). A mandate can also contribute to the organization's public image. Institutional investors believe that investing in green bonds could result in a more efficient diversification of investment portfolios and higher returns.

The survey asked local institutional investors to identify any significant barriers to investing in green bonds. Almost 50% of respondents stated

that the primary impediment is the inadequate supply of green bonds and limited green bond issuances in the local market. This clearly indicates that Malaysia's current supply of green bonds is insufficient to meet demand. As a result, there is a significant opportunity for issuers to consider green bond issuance as a means of diversifying their investor base (**Figure 11**). All of the underwriters participating in the survey indicated that attracting new investors is among the top motivations for issuers to consider a green bond issuance.

Additionally, around 15% of respondents indicated that the absence of clear benefits from investing in green bonds and the lack of internal guidance and resources for such investments are two of key inhibiting factors, while only 9% indicated that the absence of regulatory guidance on green bonds is also an impediment. As a result, it appears that local regulatory agencies have been very successful in encouraging local institutional investors to make sustainable and responsible investments.

As the majority of green bonds are issued by corporations, the majority of investors prioritize credit rating when making investment

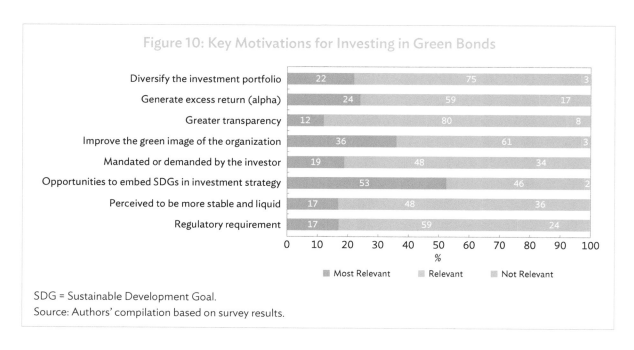

Figure 10: Key Motivations for Investing in Green Bonds

	Most Relevant	Relevant	Not Relevant
Diversify the investment portfolio	22	75	3
Generate excess return (alpha)	24	59	17
Greater transparency	12	80	8
Improve the green image of the organization	36	61	3
Mandated or demanded by the investor	19	48	34
Opportunities to embed SDGs in investment strategy	53	46	2
Perceived to be more stable and liquid	17	48	36
Regulatory requirement	17	59	24

SDG = Sustainable Development Goal.
Source: Authors' compilation based on survey results.

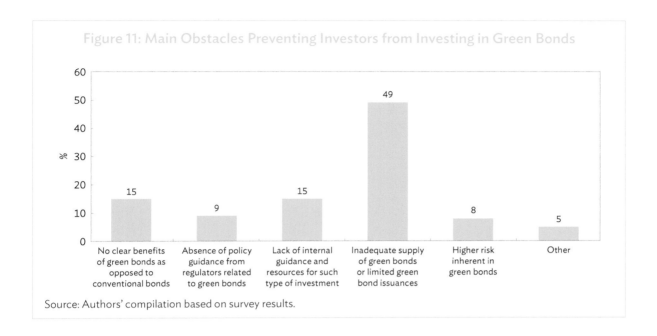

Figure 11: Main Obstacles Preventing Investors from Investing in Green Bonds

Source: Authors' compilation based on survey results.

decisions (**Figure 12**). Investors also consider the ESG impact of the bond and how the issuer intends to use the proceeds to benefit the environment as the second most important consideration. The majority of investors also believe that valuation and pricing are critical, and can aid them in making investment decisions. An external review of green bonds is one of the most crucial factors for investors to consider when making an investment decision,

according to almost 95% of respondents. Since 2020, RAM Sustainability has served as the Climate Bonds Initiative-accredited green bond verifier for Malaysia and the ASEAN region.

To address these concerns, respondents were asked to select up to three options that, in their opinion, could promote the growth of Malaysia's green bond market. Nearly 22% of responses recommended that the government

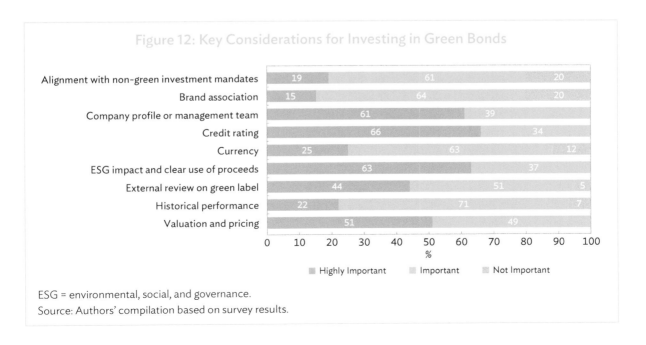

Figure 12: Key Considerations for Investing in Green Bonds

ESG = environmental, social, and governance.
Source: Authors' compilation based on survey results.

implement a standardized green taxonomy to entice investors to hold more green bonds (**Figure 13**). Meanwhile, over 21% of respondents indicated that implementing tax incentives and/or subsidies would significantly assist investors in making green investment decisions.

As previously stated, investors believe that the current domestic supply of green bonds issued in Malaysia is insufficient to meet demand, and there are numerous opportunities for prospective issuers to expand their investor base. The survey also explored which types of green bond issuers respondents would like to invest in. Local institutional investors indicated that they are most interested in sovereign green bonds, followed by issuances from financial institutions and corporate issuers (**Figure 14**).

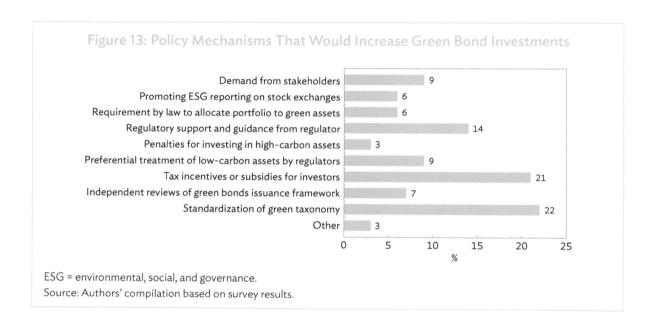

Figure 13: Policy Mechanisms That Would Increase Green Bond Investments

ESG = environmental, social, and governance.
Source: Authors' compilation based on survey results.

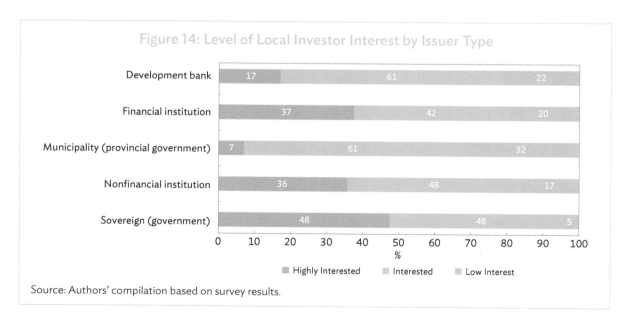

Figure 14: Level of Local Investor Interest by Issuer Type

Source: Authors' compilation based on survey results.

For corporate issuers, nearly 30% of respondents believe that the renewable energy sector offers the greatest investment potential in Malaysia, followed by energy efficiency and water management (**Figure 15**). The sector breakdown of the respondents' current portfolios of green assets is consistent with this finding.

All respondents emphasized the critical importance of government and regulatory policy clarity to increase private financing. Nearly 66% of respondents believed this to be the most important factor. Nonetheless, respondents indicated that a lack of policy clarity is not one of their primary obstacles (**Figure 16**).

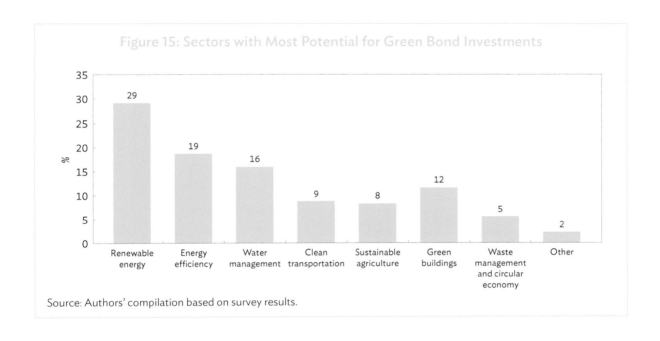

Figure 15: Sectors with Most Potential for Green Bond Investments

Source: Authors' compilation based on survey results.

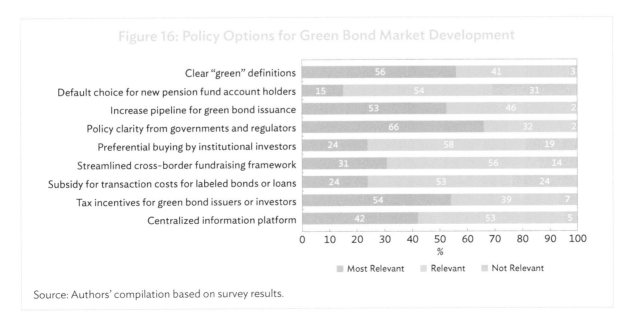

Figure 16: Policy Options for Green Bond Market Development

Source: Authors' compilation based on survey results.

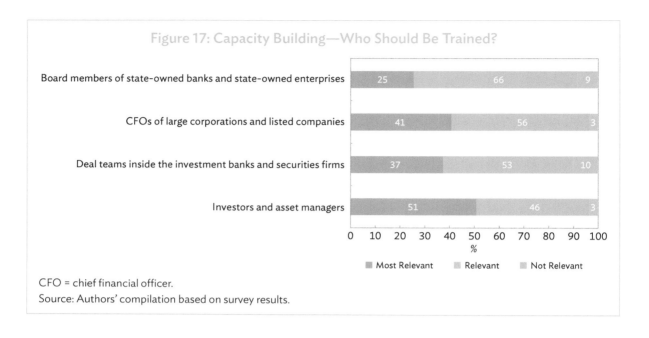

Figure 17: Capacity Building—Who Should Be Trained?

CFO = chief financial officer.
Source: Authors' compilation based on survey results.

Most investors also believed that having clear green definitions for capital markets could facilitate the mainstreaming of climate finance. This should be accompanied by an increase in the pipeline of green bond issuances so that the demand from investors can be met. Moreover, investors believed that tax incentives for issuers and investors, as well as other types of subsidies, are among the most important policy options for the government and regulatory agencies to consider.

Regarding capacity development, respondents agreed that investors themselves require additional training (**Figure 17**). This is consistent with the previous question, in which the majority of investors expressed interest in ESG investments but lacked the capacity and resources to pursue them. Similarly, deal teams within investment banks and underwriters should be trained, as they advise prospective issuers and are the key players in expanding the market's green bond supply.

When asked about their intention to invest in the region, approximately 50% of respondents indicated that they would like to do so. Singapore, Indonesia, and Thailand are the preferred investment destinations for those interested (**Figure 18**). When asked about

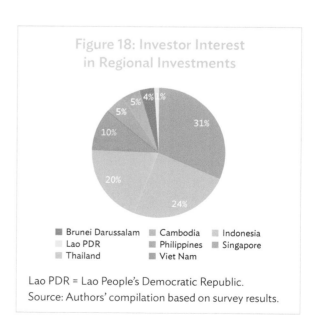

Figure 18: Investor Interest in Regional Investments

Lao PDR = Lao People's Democratic Republic.
Source: Authors' compilation based on survey results.

the underlying currency, almost 75% of respondents prefer hard currencies such as the United States dollar, euro, and Singapore dollar (**Figure 19**).

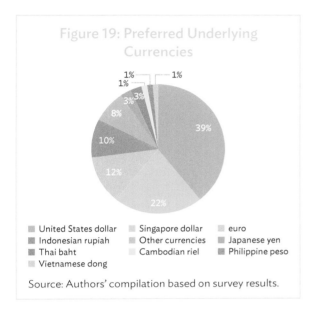

Figure 19: Preferred Underlying Currencies

- United States dollar
- Indonesian rupiah
- Thai baht
- Vietnamese dong
- Singapore dollar
- Other currencies
- Cambodian riel
- euro
- Japanese yen
- Philippine peso

Source: Authors' compilation based on survey results.

Advisors and Underwriters

This section examines the interest of potential green bond issuers, the most promising economic sectors, and the various types of potential issuers based on responses from local advisors and underwriters.

The survey began by inquiring about clients' interest in issuing green bonds. The responses indicated that their clients are generally interested in green bond issuance and are developing plans in this regard. Several clients have already issued green bonds, while others are exploring the possibility but lack the necessary resources or awareness. This may be an area where development partners such as ADB can assist interested entities with technical assistance and capacity building. This would help fill the void by increasing market issuances, thus enabling issuers to apply for the SRI Sukuk and Bond Grant Scheme. However, almost 20% of respondents indicated that their clients are not currently interested in issuing green bonds (**Figure 20**).

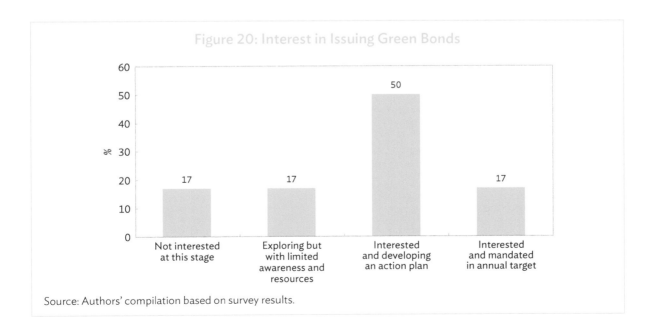

Figure 20: Interest in Issuing Green Bonds

Source: Authors' compilation based on survey results.

In terms of issuance size, 33% of respondents indicated that the optimal issuance size for green bonds ranges from USD51 million to USD100 million, and another 33% of respondents answered more than USD100 million. Meanwhile, 17% of respondents shared that the optimal deal size should be less than or equal to USD10 million and another 17% of respondents indicated USD75 million and above (**Figure 21**). More than 67% of respondents mentioned that their clients prefer issuance of green bonds in Malaysian ringgit.

Respondents indicated that renewable energy, energy efficiency, water management, and waste management and the circular economy are the sectors with the greatest potential for green bond market growth over the next 3 years (**Figure 22**). This finding is consistent with the perspectives of institutional investors, the current composition of their green asset portfolios, and the future investment potential of these sectors.

When asked why clients should issue green bonds, all respondents believe that it could improve the green image of the organization, attract new investors, and provide an opportunity

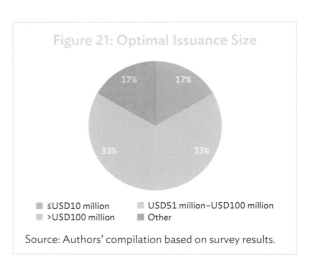

Figure 21: Optimal Issuance Size

■ ≤USD10 million   ■ USD51 million–USD100 million
■ >USD100 million   ■ Other

Source: Authors' compilation based on survey results.

to incorporate ESG as part of the corporate DNA (**Figure 23**). This is consistent with the motivations of institutional investors to invest in green bonds, particularly the opportunity for greater investment diversification. Additionally, more than 80% of respondents believed that (i) investor or lender mandates and (ii) an increase in corporate disclosure are the key drivers to increasing issuance of green bonds.

Concerning obstacles to growth, the majority of respondents identified a lack of eligible project pipelines as a clear impediment to their clients' issuing green bonds (**Figure 24**). This could

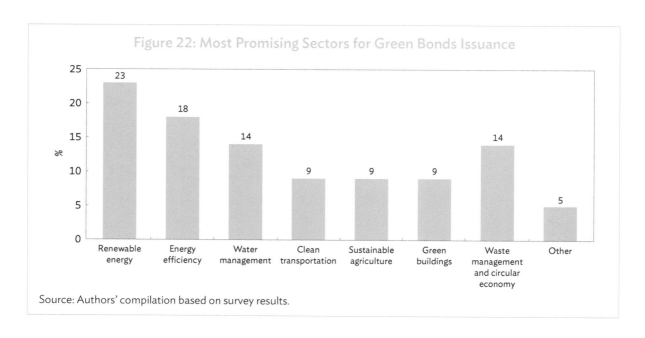

Figure 22: Most Promising Sectors for Green Bonds Issuance

Source: Authors' compilation based on survey results.

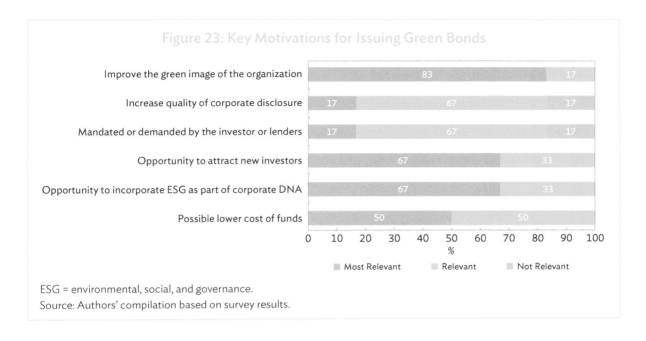

Figure 23: Key Motivations for Issuing Green Bonds

ESG = environmental, social, and governance.
Source: Authors' compilation based on survey results.

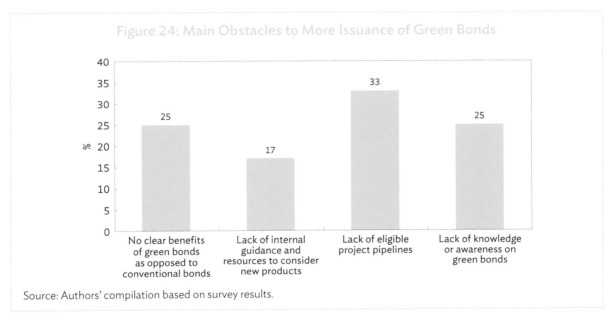

Figure 24: Main Obstacles to More Issuance of Green Bonds

Source: Authors' compilation based on survey results.

partly be due to a lack of understanding of eligible projects, assets, or expenditures that align with international and regional green bond standards and practices. Advisors and underwriters may be able to assist clients in identifying potential green projects for green bond issuance if they have a deeper understanding of how green projects are identified. Other significant impediments include the lack of awareness about green bonds as well as the absence of any clear benefit of green bonds over conventional bonds such as lower funding costs. Nonetheless, a few issuers in Malaysia have pioneered the issuance of green bonds and *sukuk*, setting a good example for other issuers to follow. For example, Cagamas Berhad, Malaysia's largest corporate bond issuer, has issued a series of sustainability bonds in the local market. **Box 2** summarizes Cagamas' experience, challenges, and observed benefits.

Cagamas Berhad (Cagamas), the National Mortgage Corporation of Malaysia, was established in 1986 by the Bank Negara Malaysia and a consortium of financial institutions as shareholders to support the national agenda of increasing home ownership and affordability through the provision of competitively priced liquidity in the secondary mortgage market in Malaysia.

Cagamas issues highly rated corporate bonds and *sukuk* (Islamic bonds) to finance the purchase of eligible housing loans from financial and nonfinancial institutions. The company is one of the largest corporate bond and *sukuk* issuers in Malaysia's capital market.

In 2019, Cagamas established the Sustainability Bond and Sukuk Framework under its MYR60 billion Medium-Term Note Programme as part of an initiative to spearhead the development of Malaysia's debt capital market and promote Islamic finance through the issuance of ASEAN Sustainability Bonds and ASEAN Sustainability SRI Sukuk. Cagamas also recognized its responsibilities to the environment and Malaysian society as affordable housing in relation to sustainable development has always been Cagamas' core priority. Hence, Cagamas' sustainability framework is a step toward reaffirming and deepening Cagamas' mission and raising awareness among the community about the importance of sustainable development— that is, development that meets the needs of the present without compromising the ability of future generations to meet their own needs.

Cagamas faced various challenges in working toward the issuance of sustainability bonds and *sukuk*. Among the early major challenges it faced were

- building awareness and changing the mindset of internal and external stakeholders,

- breaking down the complexity and eliminating misperceptions of issuance requirements and processes,
- establishing and implementing operational and reporting processes for sustainability initiatives,
- lack of industry tagging of assets to identify and secure sustainable assets,
- lack of standardized definitions of green housing and affordable housing, and
- potential noncompliance with sustainability standards that could pose reputational risk.

These challenges helped to raise awareness of sustainability among Cagamas' internal and external stakeholders. In response, Cagamas developed a Corporate Sustainability Framework to embed sustainability across its business model, operations, and planning.

To date, Cagamas has issued a total of MYR1.25 billion (USD280 million) of sustainability capital market instruments—comprising MYR700 million of ASEAN Sustainability Bonds, MYR400 million of ASEAN Sustainability SRI Sukuk, and MYR150 million of ASEAN Social SRI Sukuk—to fund the purchase of loans and financing related to affordable homes, small and medium-sized enterprises, renewable energy, and wastewater management.

From investors' perspective, asset managers are adapting and incorporating impact investing and environmental, social, and governance factors to measure investment performance, which creates growing demand for sustainability bonds and *sukuk*. Cagamas' sustainability bond and *sukuk* issuances have offered an alternative option for investors to meet their sustainable and responsible investment objectives. This can potentially result in better pricing for sustainability bond and *sukuk* issuances in the future.

Source: Cagamas.

Respondents were then asked to identify the policy mechanisms that would increase green bond issuance in Malaysia. The majority of respondents indicated that increased investor demand as well as tax incentives or subsidies for green bond issuers and investors would be the primary factor to consider, followed by preferential treatment of low-carbon assets by investors and lenders (**Figure 25**). While standardizing green taxonomies could provide clarity for green projects, only 10% of respondents identified this as a critical issue.

When asked about potential investors, nearly 70% of respondents believed that local financial institutions, fund managers, and development partners could significantly contribute to the development of the local green bond market by investing in green bonds issued by their clients. Meanwhile, all respondents agreed that insurance companies and the social security fund could also invest in green bonds (**Figure 26**).

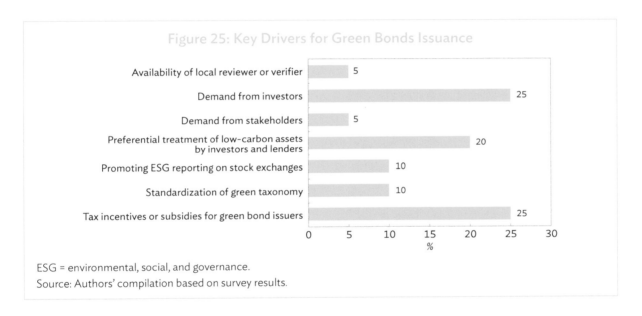

Figure 25: Key Drivers for Green Bonds Issuance

ESG = environmental, social, and governance.
Source: Authors' compilation based on survey results.

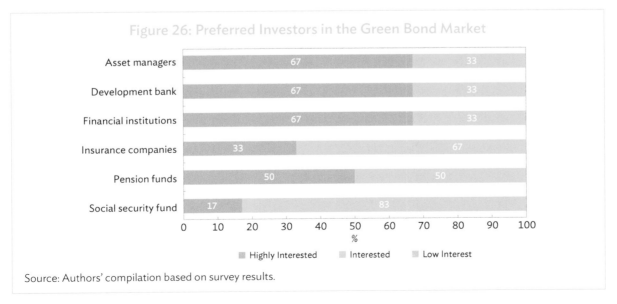

Figure 26: Preferred Investors in the Green Bond Market

Source: Authors' compilation based on survey results.

In contrast to institutional investors, underwriters and advisors believe that an increased pipeline of eligible projects for green bond issuance and preferential purchasing by central banks, pension funds, and insurance companies are necessary to further develop Malaysia's green bond market (**Figure 27**). These distinctions could be explained by the fact that local regulators, most notably the SCM and BNM, have promulgated clear regulations and guidelines to facilitate green bond issuance in Malaysia, as well as the introduction of a principle-based taxonomy that sets out guidance for financial institutions to identify green assets that may be subject to climate risks. On the other hand, underwriters and advisors may believe that local institutional investors—particularly pension funds, social security funds, and insurance companies—should communicate their commitments clearly. One good example is the introduction of the Sustainable Investment Policy of the Employees Provident Fund (EPF)

in March 2022. The policy explains the EPF's overall approach to sustainable investing and the integration of ESG factors into its investment processes.[17] As part of this initiative, the EPF will introduce a sustainable savings option to allow members to manage their investments according to their personal values.[18]

All respondents agreed that the SRI Sukuk and Bond Grant Scheme established by the SCM to encourage the issuance of SRI *sukuk* and sustainable bonds is highly relevant to the growth of the green bond and *sukuk* market in Malaysia.

In terms of capacity building, all respondents believe that investors and asset managers would benefit from training to better understand green bonds and the reason for them to be included in their investment strategy (**Figure 28**). In addition, all respondents believe that board members of state-owned enterprises should

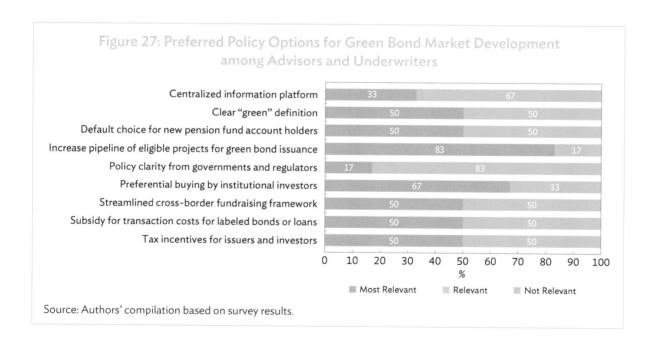

Figure 27: Preferred Policy Options for Green Bond Market Development among Advisors and Underwriters

Source: Authors' compilation based on survey results.

17   EPF. Sustainable Investment. https://www.kwsp.gov.my/about-epf/corporate-profile/sustainable-investment.

18   P. Subramaniam. 2022. EPF to launch sustainable savings option for members. *Edge Weekly*. 25 April. https://www.theedgemarkets.com/article/epf-launch-sustainable-savings-option-members.

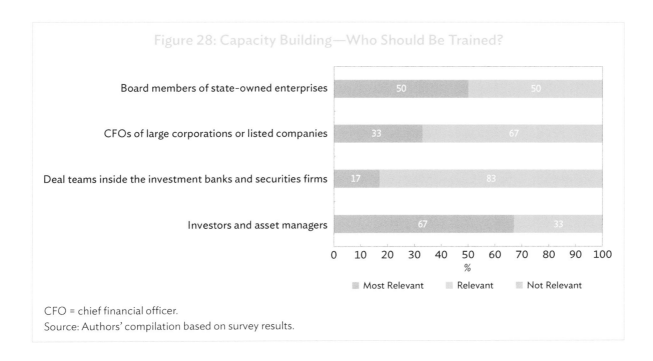

Figure 28: Capacity Building—Who Should Be Trained?

CFO = chief financial officer.
Source: Authors' compilation based on survey results.

receive training, as state-owned enterprises could serve as a leading example in promoting green bond issuances in Malaysia, thereby increasing the domestic market's supply of green bonds. All respondents agreed that deal teams within investment banks and securities firms, as well as CFOs of large corporations and listed companies, require training as well.

WHAT ADB CAN DO TO HELP

Respondents identified several ways in which ADB could assist the Malaysian green bond market's development. These beneficial recommendations can be classified as follows.

As a Knowledge Partner

The majority of respondents indicated ADB could provide technical and knowledge support to potential green bond issuers, including with the preparation of the framework, identification of projects, and development of an internal control system for monitoring of proceeds allocation and impact reporting purposes (**Box 3**).

In addition, respondents indicated that ADB should continue promoting the importance and benefits of green bonds, not only in Malaysia but throughout the region. ADB could compile successful green bond case studies and share them with potential issuers so they can consider these cases when preparing to issue a green bond.

One respondent suggested that ADB help provide clarity on the green bond issuance process and increase knowledge and awareness among relevant stakeholders in Malaysia—including potential issuers, capital market intermediaries, institutional investors, and the general public—by organizing capacity-building events in collaboration with local stakeholders in Malaysia such as relevant industry associations. In addition to organizing Malaysia-specific events, a number of respondents proposed the organization of knowledge-sharing events across ASEAN so that they can also learn from the experiences of regulators and issuers in other economies.

Information accessibility was emphasized by a number of respondents. For example, ADB could provide details on current green bond issuers and their green bond features on a centralized platform in cooperation with local regulators. Additionally, respondents suggested that ADB provide regular updates on the regional green bond market's development.

One respondent shared that ADB can help governments to design financing solutions that make infrastructure projects more bankable and accessible for private sector capital. Moreover, the respondent suggested the adoption of Islamic financing principles in green finance, which would widen the investor base for infrastructure projects.

Box 3: The Asian Development Bank's Technical Assistance to Support Malaysian Issuers and Underwriters

The Asian Development Bank (ADB) is implementing a regional technical assistance (TA) program to develop an ecosystem for sustainable local currency bond market development in Association of Southeast Asian Nations plus the People's Republic of China, Japan, and the Republic of Korea (ASEAN+3). Under the guidance of ASEAN+3 finance ministers and central bank governors, this TA was developed and implemented in accordance with the ASEAN+3 Asian Bond Markets Initiative's (ABMI) Medium-Term Road Map for 2019–2022.

The TA project's objective is to improve a sustainable finance ecosystem in the ASEAN+3 region, including Malaysia, and advance Malaysia as a regional sustainable finance hub. One of the main activities is to increase awareness of sustainable bonds among key capital market participants. In 2021, the Securities Commission Malaysia was invited to share its perspective in the keynote address at a regional webinar on scaling up sustainable finance co-organized by ADB and RAM Sustainability. The webinar aimed at creating greater awareness of green finance among local stakeholders and disseminating information on RAM Sustainability's verification service under the Climate Bonds Standards.

Another key TA activity is to provide hands-on support to prospective issuers and underwriters to facilitate the issuance of sustainable bonds in Malaysia—from identifying eligible projects, assets, and expenditures to preparing green, social, and sustainability bond frameworks and conducting discussions with external reviewers.

ADB would be happy to provide free consultation and technical hands-on support to Malaysian companies wishing to issue sustainable bonds in Malaysia or to expand fundraising opportunities around the region using green, social, or sustainable bonds.

Source: ADB.

As an Investor, Issuer, and Guarantor

ADB can also serve as an anchor investor to spur the growth of the green bond market. The respondents suggested that in addition to serving as an anchor investor, ADB should offer credit guarantees on green bonds issued by their clients. This would greatly enhance credit ratings and enable issuers to draw in new investors. One respondent mentioned the Credit Guarantee and Investment Facility as an additional potential mechanism for assisting smaller businesses with small-scale projects and limited track records in issuing green bonds.

Finally, in addition to investing in green bonds, ADB could consider providing loans to entities as a way to improve their creditworthiness before accessing the bond market.

FINAL WORD FROM SURVEY RESPONDENTS

Survey respondents were asked to give some final words on green bond market development in Malaysia. The following are a few highlights:

Supply

- A regional green bond fund that invests in renewable energy across ASEAN would be a good starting point for this region.
- There is a lack of green bond supply in the market now. The governments should encourage potential bond issuers to issue green bonds by providing them with various incentives.
- The green bond market is still very much nascent and requires a lot of effort to convince issuers to opt for green bonds (especially corporates), considering the additional cost involved and no real savings on yield in relation to conventional bonds.
- Bond market growth has been rather slow due to a lack of incentives from regulators as well as a lack of interest among the private sector.

Demand

- Regional cross-border investments should be encouraged for medium-sized banks, not just the major banks and bigger institutional funds.
- The demand side is progressing faster, which creates a mismatch between the demand for and supply of green bonds.

- The region is starting at a low base and there are tremendous opportunities and low-hanging fruit to pluck to expand the market as a proportion of total debt and capital markets. Stakeholders in both the supply and demand for green, social, and sustainability instruments will have to level up their agendas and move in tandem with stronger commitments to accelerate activities in sustainable financing.

Market Development

- The market needs increasing support, for example, by encouraging issuance of more quality rated green bonds, ensuring some liquidity (tradability), and developing a robust governance framework.
- The government's determination and contributions are very much needed in the beginning stage of stepping up a systemic and investor-friendly framework to access green and ESG issuer information.
- We need a top-down approach (i.e., clear guidelines and ESG compliance at the issuance level and a standardized rating approach for ESG compliance) if possible.
- More tax incentives are needed for the issuance of green bonds. In addition, the bond issue must have a good credit rating.
- Governments and regulators should prioritize green bonds with the benefit reflected in optimized capital charges below that of conventional bonds.

▶ Green bonds are the future as ESG is no longer optional; companies need to be ready for the issuance of green bonds.

▶ A more collaborative approach is needed to align the interests of all stakeholders, regulatory commitment, and policy options to incentivize green investment.

▶ A standardized taxonomy and disclosures for green bonds is necessary, including having an external reviewer for green labeling, as well as enhanced information on green bonds via common bond platforms.

▶ We need to work together to expedite the practice of sustainable finance for future generations.

NEXT STEPS

This survey revealed that the majority of respondents are committed to becoming more environmentally friendly, both from an investor and underwriter perspective. Meanwhile, some investors are yet to have exposure to green bonds. Thus, additional efforts are required to create more awareness and technical expertise among local stakeholders, particularly in terms of capacity building and expansion of the eligible project pipeline and issuer base. This is where development partners can play a role to support sustainable finance market development in Malaysia.

The renewable energy, water management, and energy efficiency industries currently dominate Malaysia's green bond market. In addition to having sizable positions in investor portfolios, these industries have the potential to accelerate the development of Malaysia's green bond market over the next 3 years. It is essential to assist businesses from other sectors to provide issuers with more funding options and investors with more investment opportunities.

As Secretariat of the ABMI, ADB will continue to work closely with local regulatory bodies to establish and strengthen the ecosystem necessary for Malaysia's sustainable finance market development, including capacity building, the publication of guidance notes and handbooks, and technical assistance to issuers on their sustainable finance journey.

Lightning Source UK Ltd.
Milton Keynes UK
UKHW050629170223
417164UK00031B/305

Round And About
Grenoside

by

The Grenoside & District Local History Group

Copyright © 2003
All rights reserved

First Published November 2003

ISBN 1-901587-32-0

Printed and published by
ALD
279 Sharrow Vale Road
Sheffield S11 8ZF
Tel: (0114) 267 9402
E mail: a.lofthouse@btinternet.com

INTRODUCTION

This book has been compiled by members of the Grenoside & District Local History Group. The present Group was formed five years ago when Council support for local history classes in Chapeltown & Grenoside was withdrawn.

The two classes were urged by their former tutor, Sam Sykes, to amalgamate and continue meeting. This we did and now look back somewhat surprised to record some 200 Tuesday morning meetings including about 60 outside speakers covering a wide range of subjects with an historical flavour, together with 50 visits to sites of historical interest both locally and as widespread as Skipton and Northampton.

None of us would claim to be a serious historian, but we aim to provide a regular meeting place where one can be reminded of the past, both good and bad, of an area which is full of interest. We live in an era obsessed with changing everything which is why we find it rewarding to consider and perhaps record what happened hereabout in the past.

We are fortunate that we can turn to the early works of Eastwood, Gatty & Hunter so well supplemented today by Mel Jones and David Hey. Of particular benefit is Chris Morley's "Grenoside" together with the reminiscences of Albert Goddard, Harold Wasteney and Jim Beever, plus the two books published by the Grenoside Group before the amalgamation of the two classes.

But there is still plenty of information worthy of record to illustrate why our members find it pleasing to turn up on Tuesdays to find out what happened yesteryear in a district that still doesn't see itself as just a suburb of Sheffield.

Why Grenoside and District? We meet in Grenoside but many of our members come from further afield. So we added "and District" to cover a radius of say five miles from the village but there is no rigid frontier. We tend to look away from Sheffield itself since the City has its own societies and experts. Our interests tend to lie more in the less urban country to the north and west of the City - an area which includes several villages which still retain their own character plus some beautiful unspoilt countryside.

The Group is made up of a wide range of people who all have different interests and likes.

We asked some of them to give an example of what gave them pleasure and the answers are set out in the following pages. We hope you find them as interesting and evocative as we do.

This book is dedicated to the memory of Margaret Batson whose obvious love of Grenoside and her enthusiasm for its history enriched the lives of all our members past and present.

Jim Whitham left the Angel pub on Main Street, Grenoside in 1912. We know no more than that.

The disappearance of flat caps, bowlers, whippets and heavy moustaches is unimportant but it does seem sad that none of the 38 Grenosiders can be named (so far?)

The objective of any local history group is to remember and record what happened, both good and bad, hereabouts in the past. This book is the third produced by our Group following on from "Memories of Grenoside" and "Local Heroes". We hope to carry on with this series.

We are pleased to acknowledge the excellent work done by the Chapeltown and High Green Archive whose books and exhibitions, including Grenoside, have done so much to arouse interest in this subject.

CONTENTS

1. Grenoside in the Nineteenth Century: A Comparison Between the Censuses of 1841 and 1881   *Sam Sykes*

Setting the Scene

Situated on the northern fringe of Sheffield, Grenoside could not have been oblivious to the massive changes being wrought in Sheffield throughout the nineteenth century. Here the steel industry was rapidly expanding, with the creation of enormous factory units employing hundreds and, in some cases, thousands of men. Consequent upon this was a massive increase in the town's population, composed partly of a local population explosion and partly of migration from neighbouring areas. This pattern affected not just central Sheffield but also many of the smaller townships on its fringes.

Ecclesfield parish, of which Grenoside was a part, was (according to Hunter) "where all the nails in this town are made". It was also the site of the Newton Chambers works at Thorncliffe, Chapeltown. This had first fired up in 1793 and like its Sheffield neighbours expanded quickly, creating both employment and a demand for housing. Newton Chambers also had mining interests, utilising the local mineral resources of coal and iron within their foundries. These interests created an urban development pattern typical of West Yorkshire, with new communities growing wherever the mines were sunk, often eclipsing in size older, more settled villages. Technological advances in drainage and ventilation allowed the rapid expansion of deep mines which both met and then created new industrial demand. By the mid nineteenth century numerous mining communities dotted West Yorkshire. The nearest to Grenoside were those at Thorncliffe operated by the Newton Chambers company. Mining lagged slightly behind the steel industry; the latter grew fastest in the first half of the century, coal mining waited until the second half for its greatest advances. Between the pair of them they created a monumental shift in the patterns of landscape, urban settlement and employment opportunities. The population of Ecclesfield parish increased by over 70% in the first 40 years of the century and then by a further 130% in the next 40 years.

Grenoside bordered but was not central to either the coalfield or the iron and steel factories. In the great urbanisation Grenoside was left behind, its population increase being a mere 19% between 1841 and 1881. Since the beginning of the century it had been abandoned not just by the new industry but crucially also by the new transport networks. In 1881 Grenoside was still a small discrete township of 1600 people separated from urban Sheffield by several miles of pastoral countryside. Its neighbouring communities, Ecclesfield, Chapeltown and High Green on the east, Oughtibridge on the west, and Wadsley to the south were all still villages, although rapidly undergoing an urban transformation. Indeed, Wadsley was on the verge of becoming part of the Sheffield sprawl and Ecclesfield was a centre of significant metal working industry. Only Wortley to the north retained a primarily rural character but even this township had long been the site of a small but significant forging industry which had only declined since the development of large scale steel making in Sheffield.

All around Grenoside then, the landscape was subject to significant changes brought about by intensive capital investment in the deep coal mines and steel related industries. A hitherto rural landscape was being transformed, not just by the industry itself but also by the new transport infrastructure that developed to serve the industry. A web of railways linked into cross Pennine routes via the newly constructed Woodhead tunnel. None of these railways however ran through the hilly terrain of Grenoside, they preferred the less awkward valley routes to east and west. When the Wadsley to Langsett route was turnpiked in 1805 it must have removed a great deal of traffic from the "Old Turnpike" of 1770, which had followed an ancient track through Grenoside village and along the Woodhead Road ridge route to Cheshire and the salt mines.

The Village Layout

A "New Turnpike" of 1830 attempted to partially restore the viability of the ridge route by taking a lower, less steep line than previously, just east of and below the village centre. Although this line may have reclaimed some of the traffic, it was not enough to create a new village focus. Some ribbon development did take place alongside the New Turnpike, but this primarily provided services for travellers, for example blacksmith's shops and an inn, The Red Lion, at Nether Houses. The traditional village centre, however, was sufficiently established along the old turnpike to resist any wholesale change and it has continued to develop as the focus of village life to the present day.

By 1881 the New Turnpike only linked Sheffield to the clothing towns of the North West, it had not yet taken the decisive swing north-eastwards which was to turn it into the main Sheffield to Barnsley road (the present A61). Traffic from Sheffield heading for these destinations still made its way via Chapeltown and Hoyland Common. By 1881, therefore, the new industrial traffic of the coal and steel industries had effectively bypassed Grenoside, leaving a small village isolated in the uplands.

However before the trade routes had caused its neglect, Grenoside's proximity to the Sheffield iron and steel trades had already created a definite industrial character within the village. Local legend and some documentary sources record the activities of Samuel Walker and associates in the mid eighteenth century. They were casting steel in a process soon to become famed, but only when it became housed in larger more convenient works at Masbrough, in the valley of the Don. Grenoside's upland position might have been well suited to the small scale furnaces that utilised wind power for their blast, but it was totally unsuited to the expansionist needs of large scale iron and steel production. It seems highly likely that a colony of "little mesters" began to develop around Walker's operation, taking the raw castings and developing them into finished products. No reliable occupational figures exist for the period before 1841, but it can be clearly seen by comparing the Enclosure Map of 1797 to the Ordnance Survey map of 1851 that the area now known as "The Cupola" around Walker's furnace became infilled with the houses of small scale independent metal workers. Prior to this Grenoside scarcely existed as a village in the nucleated, lowland sense. It was more of a scattering of farmsteads supplemented by commons encroachments which had formed a number of independent hamlets. Because of this, pre-nineteenth century references to the area use the term "Grenofirth", indicating a place in the woods or forest. This may seem less geographically specific but is topographically accurate.

The area which came to be known as Grenoside township (and the ecclesiastical parish of St. Mark's) radiates out from a tightly clustered village centre situated upon a crossroads. Where the ancient cross-Pennine route crossed the track which linked Ecclesfield church to its chapelry at Bradfield. Isolated farms were scattered around the parish boundaries. The eastern side, lower, sheltered and more fertile, contained several neat little hamlets, Woodseats, Barnes Green, Whitley, Wood End, Middleton Green and Creswick are all folded in between the woods and miniature river valleys. Settlements on the more exposed western side tended to remain as individual farmsteads, as at Stubbin, Little Intake and Skew Hill, rather than growing into hamlets. By 1841, however, the vast bulk of the population was concentrated into two quadrants immediately north-west and north-east of the crossroads at the village centre.

In 1881, after almost a century of industrial development, the village contained 354 households, 66 of which (around 20%) were in the eastern hamlets. That these were of a different character to the main village be easily seen from a comparison of occupations within the different geographical sectors (Table 1). Unfortunately the boundaries of these sectors do not coincide with those of the natural hamlets, nonetheless we can clearly see that over half of all the agricultural workers lived within just 3 of the 10 divisions: Foster Houses, Whitley and Wood End; whilst over half of all the metal finishing workers lived in 3 other sectors: Cupola, Lump Lane and Nether Houses.

Table 1   1881 census for Grenoside: occupations by geographical sector

| Area | Occupation | | | | | | | | |
	Iron & Steel	Metal finishing workers	Coal	Land	Service	Stone	Crafts	Prof.	Total
Cupola	2	31	3	5	3	15	0	0	59
Lump Lane	6	27	7	2	6	20	4	1	73
Nether Houses	4	27	1	7	8	0	9	2	58
Wood Nook	4	18	4	3	2	10	1	0	42
Foster Houses	4	18	3	18	6	1	2	0	52
Skew Hill	3	15	0	6[a]	0	7	2	2	11
Norfolk Lane	6	11	8	1	12	10	2	3	53
Old Turnpike[b]	0	10	5	0	0	13	4[c]	2	34
Wood End	9	6	6	11	16	3	1	2	54
Whitley	6	5	0	20	11	3	0	0	45
Total	44	168	37	83	64	83	23	12	514

a   4 of these were dual occupation "farmer/shuttle tip & spring maker".
b   Included 8 grocers/shopkeepers/innkeepers.
c   1 of these was a dual occupation "Publican & Cordwainer".

The Old Turnpike retained a concentration of commercial services whilst those areas which recorded the highest numbers of workers in the coal mines and the iron and steel foundries were, predictably, those situated en route to Chapeltown and High Green, site of the Newton Chambers works.

The cottage industrialists were almost all concentrated into a mish-mash of narrow streets north of the crossroads, spanning either side of the old turnpike. Of the 10 registration districts isolated in the 1881 census, the "inner circle" contained around two thirds of all the metal finishers. Contemporary Ordnance Survey maps and the extant street pattern confirm that this was a densely populated area of higgledy-piggledy housing and workshops, infilling between the main access roads.

The Economic Structure and Overall Changes

Table 2   Overall Changes in Grenoside 1841-1881

	1841	1881	% change
Households	291	324	+11
Population: male	692	824	+19
female	679	783	+12
total	1371	1607	+15
Average size of household	5	4.9	
Average number of children per family	3.5	3.3	
% heads of households who were female	11%	15%	+4
Houses with servants	45	29	-36
Houses with lodgers	74	74	

Already by 1841 metal trades formed a significant part of the Grenoside economy. Almost half of all the occupations recorded were metal related, mostly in some form of finishing trade, only 3% were involved in the primary manufacturing process. Such mono-industrial concentration was not unusual, indeed in many villages it was of a higher proportion and around Sheffield at this time most of the rural villages echoed to the sound of one or the other iron trades as each area developed its own speciality. The most dominant trade within Grenoside was file cutting, which accounted for about half of all those working in the metal trades. A further quarter of all metal workers were making nails, a business for which Ecclesfield parish had long been famous. This was almost exclusively male work, only one female being recorded out of 178 metal workers. However, this may have been in part a failure to record female labour that was part-time, seasonal or only used sporadically as markets or labour requirements demanded.

Extract from a census return for Ecclesfield

Table 3   Changes in Occupations in Grenoside 1841-1881

	1841			1881			% change since 1841
	Males	Females	Total	Males	Females	Total	
Metal Trades: files	82	0	82	87	8	95	+16
all	186	1	187	195	17	212	+13
Land: farmers	35	1	36	22	4	26	-28
ag. labs.	46	0	46	21	0	21	-54
woodmen	11	0	11	3	0	3	-73
all	91	1	92	78	5	83	-10
Domestic	20	48	68	10	54	64	-6
Crafts: shoemakers	14	0	14	7	0	7	-50
dressmakers	0	4	4	0	7	7	+75
all	24	5	29	18	7	25	-14
Stone: masons	15	0	15	10	1	11	-27
all	16	0	16	81	2	83	+419
Education	5	3	8	4	1	5	
Mining	6*	0	6	32	0	32	+433
Shops & Pubs	3	1	4	13	5	18	
Labourers	4	0	4	7	0	7	
Transport	2	0	2	7	1	8	
Building	0	0	0	5	0	5	
Manufacturers/ Owners	3	1	4	4	1	5	
Professionals	2	0	2	4	0	4	
General	6	0	6	4	0	4	
Independent	5	6	11	0	0	0	
Apprentices unspecified	3	0	3	0	0	0	
Total	376	66	442	462	93	555	+25

* 3 of these were ironstone

By 1881 the number of employed people in Grenoside had risen by around 12% and the metal related trades had more or less held their market share of employees, losing just 3% of the total workforce to other areas. With the exception of Joseph Ashton, Shuttle Tip manufacturer of New Middle Lane who employed 18 men, most of these workers appear to have been self-employed, working with their immediate family or an apprentice.

The most significant change in the metal working arena was the total loss of nailmaking as a trade. It seems likely that as this process became more mechanised and centred upon the larger factories the former practitioners diversified into other metal finishing trades, like shuttle-tip manufacture and spindle making. Both of these trades were insignificant in 1841 but noteworthy in 1881.

The number of females recorded in metal trades also changed significantly by1881. As gross numbers, 8 female file cutters and 9 women in miscellaneous trades, were not essential to the industrial workforce, but these trades did represent the second most important source of female employment opportunity. In most instances there appears to have been some family connection between the female metal worker and her husband or father, connection which raises the suspicion that even increased numbers may under represent the actual numbers of females who gave service to the metal trades, however temporary.

These bare statistics offer but a glimpse of the human cost of file cutting employment and whilst the chronic illnesses associated with the grinding trades have been well documented, file cutters do not appear to have received the same attention. Table 4 however demonstrates vividly this human cost by comparing the ages of file cutters to those of agricultural workers.

Table 4   Ages of File Cutters and Agricultural Labourers in Grenoside 1841-1881

Occupation	Age (years) 14-19	20-29	30-39	40-49	50-59	60+	Total
File Cutters							
1841	22	26	12	17	4	3	84
1881	15	24	18	9	5	4	75
Agricultural Labourers							
1841	5	8	6	5	4	2	30
1881	2	12	5	11	4	11	45

In both cases the owners and farmers have been excluded to avoid distortion. It can be clearly seen that a file cutter aged 50 years or over was a rare being indeed, only around 10% of file cutters were still active at this age. In farming, on the other hand, over a third of the agricultural workforce are aged over 50 years. Either agricultural workers, despite their relatively low pay and status, enjoyed healthier working conditions, or else agricultural labour was a source of employment for file cutters too incapacitated to work in their trade. There is no evidence to support the latter, and indeed common sense argues against it, for agricultural labour must have been at least as arduous as file cutting. However it is just possible that a transfer from file cutting to farm work accounts for the absolute decline in aged file cutters and a commensurate increase in elderly farm labourers.

No other trade or industry offered numerical competition to metal working. Grenoside's semi-rural location demanded an agricultural infrastructure and in 1841 agriculture accounted for 24% of all workers. In line with national trends, this had fallen by 1881 but at just over 15%, agricultural employment was still more significant here than it was elsewhere in the locality. In High Green, for instance, the proportion had declined to around 3% by 1881. The decline was not uniform across the range of agricultural occupations however. The number of people recorded as "Farmer" had fallen sharply by around one-third, from 35 to 22 and this probably represented some rationalisation and amalgamation of farmsteads, for there was little decline in the gross amount of land devoted to agriculture. The number of labourers employed however fell by over half from 46 in 1841 to 21 in 1881, a much greater rate of decline that must have been caused jointly by changing personal horizons and the changes in practice brought about by technological advancement and the increasing move away from arable farming. The relatively higher wages on offer in the new industries must have sucked local labour off the land in much the same way as it attracted labour from the rural counties of the south and east midlands. One particular agriculturally related trade, that of woodman, had been reduced even more dramatically, from 11 workers in 1841 to just 3 in 1881. Again this must indicate a change in practice, for the extensive woodland area continued to be managed. These statistics show that agricultural employment was a male preserve in 1841 that had been scarcely breached 40 years later, only one woman, the aged widow Heward is described as a farmer. However, like their sisters in the metal trades, many farm wives and daughters might have raised an eyebrow at their exclusion from the records.

Because of the different accounting methods employed and, in some instances, the different self descriptions given to the enumerator, it is not possible to make absolute comparisons between the 1841 and 1881 censuses. The former does not include any assessment of acreage, whilst the latter fails to include such assessments in some cases and it is sometimes difficult to tell whether a farm has changed its name or the farmer has moved premises. Nonetheless Table 5 attempts to show those farms, around two-thirds of the whole, where there was some continuity across the latter half of the century. In a few cases we see mobility, the Brownhills of Woodseats are agricultural labourers in the 1841 census but 40 years later have either earned the right or gained the audacity to call themselves farmers, albeit on only 24 acres. At Cinder Hill however, Harry Jackson has led his family in the opposite direction, whilst his father claimed to be a farmer, Harry pretends to be no more than a farm labourer. The fact that he has no acreage recorded supports his description.

The dominant female employment throughout this period was domestic service, not so much a career as a rite of passage through which future mothers must graduate. Over two-thirds of all female employees were "in service", the majority as unspecified servants but a few, mainly the older ones who had perhaps by design or default made this into a career, were designated "housekeeper", "laundress" or "cook". The proportions are remarkably consistent across the period under study, what is surprising however is the decline of male servants in the same period, the real number actually halved, from 20 to 10, and this at a time of population increase. No doubt the new industries offered more affluent prospects than traditional servitude.

Domestic service and dressmaking were the only occupational sectors where women outnumbered the men. In 1881 a reasonably large number of women (17) were employed in the metal trades, but these were primarily wives or daughters in the employment of a family member.

Table 5   The Farmers in Grenoside:

Families or Individuals in Continuous Occupation 1841-1881

Farm	1841	1881	Acres
Green Lane	John Heward	Elizabeth Heward	80
Hall Field Head	George Wood	George Wood	72
Hill Top	George Unwin sr.	George Unwin jr.	69
Hunter House	William Stanley sr.	William Stanley jr.	65
Holme Lane	David Loxley sr.	David Loxley jr.	58
Hill Top	John Boler	John Boler	40
Hoyle House	Joseph Taylor	Fred Taylor	38
Woodseats	John Brownhill sr. (Ag. Lab.)	John Brownhill jr.	24
South Whitley	Ben Johnson	James Johnson	20
Cinder Hill	Stephen Jackson	Harry Jackson	(Farm Lab.)
Intake	Reuben Ibbotson	Thos. Ibbotson	
Middleton Green	John Rider	John Rider	(Retired)

Farms Changing Names

Farm	1841		1881	Acres
Cross House	John Smith	Lane Head House	Joseph Smith	56
Greno Wood Head	Thomas Marshall	Nether Houses	Frances Marshall	
Grenoside	Barnett Eyre (Ag. Lab.)	Whitley	Isaac Eyre	53
The Hurst	George Gill sr.	Middleton Green	Geo. Gill jr.	23

Farms Disappearing

Oughtibridge Hall	Joseph Smith
Woodseats	John Johnson
Wheel	Henry Froggat
Creswick	Thomas Loxley

Farms Changing Families

Farm	Acres
Sycamore Lodge	23
Whitley	20
Whitley	20
Skew Hill	11
Skew Hill	10
Whitley	8
Sycamore Cottage	8
Hoyle House	7

	1841	1881
Total Farmers	34	25 (+ 2 retired)
Ag. Labs	46	16

Probably of more economic significance were those handful of women recorded as farmers, or publicans. These were normally widows who had presumably inherited the business upon the death of a husband rather than having acquired it through their independent entrepreneurial activity. Such a potentially sexist statement needs explanation. For example, in 1841 John Heward, age 35 years, is the farmer of Green Lane; 40 years later it is his widow, Elizabeth, age 78, who is recorded as farmer. This is not to say of course that Elizabeth, or any of the other women in a similar position, had not previously played a major part in running the enterprise.

Dressmaking was the only craft in which women figured, but the reasonably high figure (7 in 1881) gives no indication as to whether this was organised out-work for a factory, or purely supplying the local needs. Although a linen manufacturer resided in the village there was no evidence to suggest that he invested locally. Indeed the similar statistics derived from neighbouring High Green suggest that this was not so. Curiously the male counterpart, tailoring, does not register at all. All the other trades are much as we would expect in a village that would have been partially self-sufficient. It is worth noting however that not a single baker was to be found in the village. This was still presumably a domestic task. One would expect a rural village to be well supplied with the craftsmen necessary for self-sufficiency. This held more or less true across the period, but with some significant features. Blacksmiths, shoemakers and dressmakers were the most significant crafts, with the latter being the only opportunity for females to practise a skilled trade, save for one "thread spinner" recorded in 1841. Shoemakers suffered the greatest change, declining from 14 in 1841 to 7 in 1881. This almost certainly equates with the national trend towards concentrating shoe production in the south midlands, where mass production techniques combined with improved rail transport to make national marketing a reality. Why did the same not apply to dressmaking? Grenoside is not alone in the continuance of this totally female home-based trade.

Another significant change in village social and economic life is shown by the dramatic increase in the number of shopkeepers and publicans, from 4 to 18. This trend is consistent with national developments towards the establishment of local shops in opposition to traditional markets. The supply of goods to local shops being supported by an improved transport network, this factor too is shown at Grenoside in a four-fold increase in the number of carriers within the village.

The most significant change of all was one that affected not just the gross numbers of employees but the landscape and social scene too. In 1841 Grenoside had 16 people employed in the stone trades, all bar one of which were described as "masons". Forty years later there were 83 stone workers, including just 11 masons. The rest were directly employed in quarrying the stone. It is often difficult to separate the stone masons, working with quarried stone, from the stone getters who cut and blasted the raw material in the quarries. The 1841 figure may have included some quarrymen, although these are not so defined. However, it is just as likely to have included workers with more general skills in the building trade, 5 builders are recorded in 1881 but there are no equivalent trades defined earlier. Even if there were some quarries in 1841, these could only have been small scale, whereas by 1881 outcrops would be visible all around Grenoside. The quarry workers themselves were in the main from Ecclesfield parish, although over a fifth had migrated considerable distances. They included not just employees but some small scale capitalists who employed their colleagues.

Few people in Grenoside worked for large scale employers. We have already seen that the metal workers tended towards self-employment and that the farms were relatively small concerns, however the stone quarrying and finishing trades (dressers and masons) were dominated by small scale capitalists. Typical of these were:

"Farmer & Quarry owner employing 12 men" (Stanfield Ash)
"Farmer employing 6 men & 1 boy" (Hollow Farm)
"Stone mason employing 9 men and 22 boys (Old Turnpike)
"Quarry owner employing 14 men" (Back Lane)
"Quarry owner employing 3 men" (Skew Hill)

The census entries make it difficult to distinguish between masons employed by or at a quarry and those who may have been self-employed craftsmen in the building trade. For example, Thomas Beever, the stone mason described above as an employer of 9 men, must have been much more than a jobbing builder. His son "Alban" however is described as a stone dresser, an occupation we might otherwise associate with the quarries. Overall, stone quarrying and its related trades, with around one-sixth of the total male workforce, represented a significant industry in Grenoside by the end of the nineteenth century.

The sort of small scale capitalist found in the stone trades rarely appears elsewhere, in 1881 the only other significant employers recorded are:

"Retired solicitor with 5 servants & a teacher" (Barnes Hall)
"Bus proprietor employing 1 man, 2 boys and wife" (Old Turnpike)
"Blacksmith employing 3 men & 1 boy" (Nether Houses)
"Wood merchant employing 2 men" (New Middle Lane)

A Cook and 2 Housemaids were resident at the Norfolk Arms and probably employed there but otherwise the large contingents of domestic servants were employed in small scale operations, as were the bulk of farm workers. Both these groups were concentrated in the outlying areas of the village, where both the farms and larger houses predominated.

By this time the trend to occupational specialisation was well established and few dual occupations survive. Where instances are recorded they appear to be a hangover from the days of farmers diversifying for survival. At Skew Hill we have a whole family recorded as farmers and shuttle tip and spring makers, and elsewhere a farmer and quarry owner, and a farmer and cow keeper.

Stability and mobility in 1881

Table 6 shows the number of individuals employed in each trade who were born outside the parish of Ecclesfield. It is only possible to show this figure for 1881 as the 1841 census did not record this information. There are three distinctive features here:
a) the crafts (including metal working) were dominated by indigenous workers;
b) the less skilled trades were dependant upon migrant labour;
c) the village was absolutely reliant upon outsiders for capital and professional skills.

Less than 10% of all metal workers came from outside the parish and only 4% were attracted from far afield. These were clearly skills honed to perfection within the village environment, difficult for strangers to either acquire or be accepted into the trade. The majority of immigrant file cutters came from immediately adjacent parishes where similar skills or personal relationships could have provided the entry key. This contrasts markedly with the stone industry, where at least a third of all workers were born outside the parish and over one fifth of whom came from above twenty miles away. The domestic services attracted outsiders in a very similar percentage, well over a third being immigrants and 20% from distant parts.

Perhaps most surprising of all for adherents to the theory of rural stability is the migratory pattern of land workers. Over half of all agricultural labourers were immigrants, the vast majority having been born in excess of twenty miles away. Even amongst the farmers themselves, that backbone of the rural community, as many as 20% of them had travelled considerable distances from their birthplace.

An even more mobile picture is presented by the lesser occupations. That general labouring jobs and miscellaneous trades should have been taken up by incomers is not unusual, and it is perhaps fitting that those people associated with transport should be travellers. Nonetheless it is surprising to find that 5 of 8 carriers and leaders came from outside the parish. Only one of 5 teachers was a native, 3 of the 4 professionals were outsiders and every single manufacturer or owner who now resided within the village had originated outside of it. Even in the traditional crafts, almost a quarter of the craftsmen were immigrants. On this basis one can most definitely say that the enterprise culture had not permeated Grenoside. Its employment pattern shows a deeply conservative nature with little evidence of the "local boy makes good" syndrome.

As migrants played so large a part in the local economy it is worth profiling a few of those who came to be counted. Whilst it is fair to say that the majority moved only in limited circles of relatively small compass, there were clearly some for whom travelling had become a way of life, though whether this was by choice or necessity the census cannot tell us. Nancy Nuttall for example, was 61 years old and the Licensed victualler of the Old Harrow. She had been born at Crow Edge, Cheshire, close to the important cross Pennine turnpike route that eventually fed into Grenoside's main street. She was no doubt related to two other Nuttal families recorded at Grenoside but who were born at Woodhead, Cheshire, just down the road from Crow Edge. However, Nancy did not take a direct ride down the road to Grenoside, for although her eldest son was born in Cheshire, his younger sister and brother were registered in "Scotland". Another migrant, Samuel Helton, aged 35, had been born in Nottinghamshire and had taken a wife, Ann, five years his junior, from a nearby village.

However, by the time Ann was 19 they were living in Swinton, South Yorkshire, where their first child was born. Three years later baptism records show that they had made the enormous trek south to Hampshire, only to return to Rotherham in South Yorkshire within two years. They stayed there for at least another three years where their third and fourth children were born, and had possibly not long before removed to Grenoside, for their fifth and youngest child was born in Ecclesfield parish just four months before the 1881 census.

Another wanderer with a hint of mystery is Thomas Nightingale, a 40 year old quarry man hailing from Crich in Derbyshire who had apparently appeared in Ecclesfield parish some 16 years earlier when he fathered a child called William Butler. Presumably Nightingale didn't marry the child's mother but left William with the brand of illegitimacy whilst he continued his journey north, at least as far as Barrow-in-Furness, where within four years he had met, married and impregnated Mary, a lass seven years older than himself. They had a second child the following year and then upped again. This time Thomas took his family with him.

Table 6   1881 census for Grenoside: Migration and Occupation

Trade		Males	Females	Total	Immigrants (born outside Ecclesfield parish)		
					within 20 miles	over 20 miles away	Total
Metal Trades	all	195	17	212	9	8	17
	file cutters	87	8	95	7	3	10
Stone Quarries	all	81	2	83	11	16	27
	masons	10	1	11	2	1	3
Land	all	78	5	83	6	19	25
	farmers	22	4	26	5	5	10
	farm labourers	21	0	21	2	10	12
Domestic	all	10	54	64	13	13	26
	general servant	2	20	22	9	4	13
Coal	all	32	0	32	5	4	9
	miners	28	0	28	5	3	8
Crafts	all	18	7	25	2	4	6
	dressmaker	0	7	7	1	0	1
	shoemaker	7	0	7	0	2	2
	blacksmith	6	0	6	1	1	2
Shops	all	13	5	18	2	2	4
	grocers	5	1	6	1	1	2
	publicans	4	2	6	1	1	2
Labourers		7	0	7	1	4	5
Transport		7	1	8	5	0	5
Building		5	0	5	0	2	2
Education		4	1	5	3	1	4
Manufacturers /Owners		4	1	5	2	3	5
Professionals		4	0	4	2	1	3
General		4	0	4	1	3	4
Total		462	93	555	62	80	142

Two more children were born to the couple in County Durham before they moved south. Perhaps Thomas had come to retrieve his eldest, illegitimate child? We shall likely never know the reasons but at any rate, William Butler now joined the family group as eldest son. William had a trade, boot and shoe maker, and it is possible that although his father now worked in the stone quarries he too had a previous trade or occupation in the heavy metal industry, for his trek north from Derbyshire to Barrow was almost certainly parallel to the movements of Charles Camell's engineering works. Will we ever know why Thomas turned his back?

Our final short portrait of a migrant is that of John Green, a local man who travelled and returned and, unusually for an outsider, gained employment as a file maker. Presumably his local knowledge (and possibly experience) were to his advantage. John was born in Tankersley and married a Sheffield woman, Eliza, seven years his junior. They had resided in Ecclesfield parish in 1857 when their eldest daughter was born, but by 1863 had moved to Kirkstall in Leeds. That this was another engineering centre suggests that John may well have taken his trade with him. He was still in Leeds (though not Kirkstall) in 1868 but by 1872 had once again settled in Ecclesfield parish. The eldest son, William, followed his dad into the metal trades, but as a stove grate fitter, not a file maker.

Immigrants then played a significant and possibly colourful part in Grenoside's economy, making up a quarter of the workforce, providing much of the unskilled labour and all of the capital and professional expertise within the village.

Sources

Census records for Grenoside, 1841 and 1881.

Revd. J. Hunter, *Hallamshire* (ed. Revd. A. Gatty, London, 1869).

2. Querns   *Nev Hayward*

A quern.

Introduction

The word quern has several derivations, for example; Anglo-Saxon … cwyrn; or qvairnus … Gothic; or Old English … cweorn; and perhaps phonetically nearest to our pronunciation, the Dutch … kweern.

What is a quern you may ask, as it is a word not in common use today. A quern is in fact, a simple hand mill for grinding corn, usually consisting of two stones resting one upon the other.

There are two fundamental types, saddle querns (Figure 1) and rotary querns (Figure 2). Hand stones continued in use into the Middles Ages even though water powered mills using larger stones (millstones) were introduced during the Roman period and wind power (windmills) came into use in the twelfth century.

Figure 1.   *Saddle quern...*
            Bronze and earliest Iron Ages

Figure 2.   *Rotary quern...*
            Later Iron Age and Roman Periods

Quern History

From earliest times there were no settled populations. Man was nomadic, roaming from place to place in search of food and shelter as the seasons changed. These wanderers would have been in small groups of family or close friends, probably no more than a dozen in number.

The New Stone Age heralded change, man began to settle in the more fertile areas, domesticating animals; cattle, sheep, etc., for food and work. He cultivated the land, sowing seeds and harvesting the crops.

Egyptian culture was well established in the Nile valley by 5000 BC (Neolithic/New Stone Age period). Here peas, lentils, barley and wheat were grown. Kamut, claimed to be the oldest grain of all, is said to have come from a Pharaoh's tomb and a handful of grains were taken to America where it is still cultivated on a small scale. Once harvested the cereals had to be threshed, which meant beating the "grass" until the grains separated from the stalks and husks. The grain was then winnowed – tossed into the air until the heavier grains fell to the ground and the lighter straw and husks, or chaff, blew away (Figure 3).

Figure 3.   .... Harvesting

.... *threshing*   .... *Winnowing*   .... *grinding into flour.*

The grain then had to be crushed using a Saddle Quern (see Figure 1). The simplest form of which comprised a base stone, which was usually flat or slightly concave, onto which a small quantity of grain was placed. It was then ground by rubbing a large pebble or cylindrical stone over it. A cylindrical top stone is displayed in the Tolson Museum, Huddersfield, it is thought to date from the Neolithic period (new Stone Age, 3000 – 2000 BC).

Exact dating is difficult, but in 1922 Lord Carnarvon and Howard Carter discovered the tomb of Tutankhamen in the Valley of the Kings at Luxor in Egypt. It was almost untouched by tomb robbers and the fine contents included many works of art and Tutankhamen's gold coffin. Tutankhamen became King of Egypt at an early age, probably being no more than eleven years old. He reigned from c.1360 to c.1350 BC. Many of the artefacts discovered in the tomb dated from much earlier. One item brought out was a stone sculpture depicting a servant knelt over a saddle quern crushing grain for the purpose of brewing.

The Egyptians are also thought to have been the first people to grind wheat into flour rather than just crushing it. For this they devised the Rotary Quern (see Figure 2), although this is often ascribed to the Romans.

Roman legions, led by Julius Caesar, landed on British soil in 55 BC and 54 BC and it is possible that they introduced the quern to Britain during the second stage of their invasion, although they were repelled. (However, I have seen it suggested that rotary querns were in use in Britain as early as the 3rd century BC but have been unable to find anything to substantiate this during my researches.) During the next century there was a peaceful Roman penetration of Britain, much of the southern areas being under the rule of Cunobelin. When he died his kingdom collapsed. It was in AD 43 that the Roman Emperor Claudius sent an army to conquer and add Britain to the Roman Empire.

About AD 54 the Romans constructed a fortress at Templeborough, between Sheffield and Rotherham. The principle war between the Romans and the defending Brigantes was ongoing between AD 71 and 85 and it was probably during this period that the Romans built another fort at Brough which lies between Hope and Castleton. (Part of a quern was found at Brough during excavations for the New Close Estate.) During their period of occupation, approximately 400 years, the Romans constructed a number of roads, one linked Templeborough with Brough and continued to Buxton.

As the Roman empire expanded across Europe they discovered the large Neidermendig basalt lava stone quarries in the Mayen region of Germany. This stone was found to be ideal for the manufacture of querns.

Excavations at a number of sites of known Roman settlement in this country have unearthed numerous partial or complete quern stones, many of Neidermendig lava stone, as well as in some areas, quern remains manufactured from other types of stone, see chart.

Contact Museum	Stone type		
	Neidermendig	Local	Pennine
Arberia Roman Fort & Museum	✓	✓	
Bury St. Edmunds (Suffolk County)	✓	✓	✓
Canterbury - Royd Museum	✓	✓	✓
Chesterfield	✓		✓
Colchester	✓	✓	
Epping Forest	have querns but unclassified		
Exeter City	✓		
Gloucester City	✓	✓	✓
Greater Manchester	✓		✓
Leicester		✓	✓
Lincolnshire City & County	have querns but unclassified		
London	✓		✓
Ribchester	✓	✓	
Rotherham	have querns but unclassified		
St. Albans	✓	✓	✓
St. Edmundsbury (West Stow)	✓		

This study is ongoing but there is sufficient evidence for this monograph to proceed.

As the chart shows, there have been "finds" of Neidermendig querns over most of the country where the Romans encamped or settled. This suggests the querns were carried with them as part of their domestic equipment. Once settled they no doubt experimented with any locally found stone, if suitable it would have been beneficial to make querns locally in preference to importing from Germany.

Evidence of "local stone" used is determined from excavated remains of querns and subsequent examination:

Arberia	a local sandstone (South Shields).
Canterbury	argillaceous lower greensand from local Thanet beds
Colchester	Hertfordshire puddingstone (a conglomerate) and Devonian conglomerate
St. Albans	Hertfordshire puddingstone
Suffolk	Hertfordshire puddingstone

When a local stone has been stated in the chart, but no definition given above, it is because to date, there has been no spectroscopic examination of the remains to determine type and source.

In Colchester there is evidence of imported German querns until at least the end of the 2nd century AD. Maybe the fact that sea transport was so much cheaper than overland at this time. Colchester being on the river Colne that flows to the North Sea. In London, querns dating from the Roman period, AD 250 – 400, have been found, these also being German imports. The river Thames this time offering a direct sea route.

Querns of pennine stone have been unearthed in places such as Gloucester, London, Manchester and St. Albans but without specialist examination cannot be traced to Wharncliffe, one of the sites within the Sheffield area where there is strong evidence of quern manufacture. The other being Don Bank in the Rivelin Valley.

Wharncliffe Quern Factory

Wharncliffe or more simply Quern cliff. A document, dated 1265, amongst the Wharncliffe papers held in Sheffield Archives, shows the spelling "Qwernecliff". This, I think, substantiates the derivation of the name for this area. It also implies that people recognised this as a former quern manufacturing site.

Figure 4. Quern "roughs" can be found both at high and low level in the vicinity, known as Wharncliffe Heath.

Archaeology, combining with ever advancing scientific support is used to good effect in the study of man's past. From Roman times onward there is some written evidence to support the findings of the archaeologist. A lot of information may be gleaned from controlled excavation of sites known to have been the scene of human activity. Villages and battlefields are examples. Each site is unique and unless fully recorded during excavation, evidence may be lost for ever. Sometimes groups of similar objects, originating from the same cultures become evident at a number of different excavated sites. Querns come into this category.

Since the Second World War there has been a significant increase of interest in archaeological surveys and digs. This has seen an increasing number of querns or "partials" discovered.

These discoveries prompted research into where and how these querns, made from local stone, may have been manufactured and from which area, and in fact which quarry, the stone originally came. Quern quarries have been discovered all around the country. For example, Goathland in north Yorkshire, where five upper stones were discovered. Lodsworth quarry near Midhurst in West Sussex, where querns at different stages of manufacture have been discovered. In the Bristol area several quarries of possible prehistoric and Roman date have been related to querns found on archaeological sites in the region. Only a few roughouts were found at the quarries and only rough flaking activities were recognisable.

In 1949, in a Sheffield newspaper, there appeared a short column headed "Traces of Roman Work Found". This was the first public announcement of Leslie Butcher's discovery of traces of Roman or pre Roman sites for manufacturing querns on a 150 acre site along Wharncliffe Crags, in the vicinity of the area known locally as Wharncliffe Heath.

With permission from Lord Wharncliffe, Butcher spent three seasons digging in the area and discovered, he claimed, over 1000 quern stones and some 600 working areas determined by finds of chippings. Some of the early querns from this area are thought to date from about 50 BC.

Figure 5. Flat rotary quern stones are of variable size, ranging from 350-500mm. in diameter and from 75-125mm. in thickness, with no apparent relationship between diameter and thickness.

Figure 6. The Beehive quern stones to be found at the Wharncliffe site are also of variable size: 300-400mm diameter and of similar height.

Figure 7. Butcher discovered hundreds of querns at the Wharncliffe site in various stages of manufacture and many can still be seen today.

There is a display of "Beehive" querns in various stages of manufacture in Weston Park Museum, Sheffield. It refers to the Wharncliffe site. "Beehive" quern because of the distinctive shape of the top stone. This type of rotary quern is typical of the "roughs" to be seen at Wharncliffe.

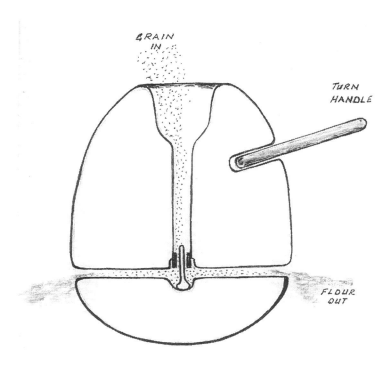

GRAIN IN

TURN HANDLE

FLOUR OUT

Figure 8. The lower stone of the pair was often flat but sometimes had a convex form as shown here. This permitted the stone, when set into soil or sand, to be at an angle yet remain stable in operation. In the hands of experienced craftsmen the crude tools, such as stone or flint axes, used to work the stone proved very effective, but surely hard work.

Between Wharncliffe and Wortley, Butcher also discovered remains of six settlements that could possibly have been associated with the quern workings. The newspaper article, mentioned earlier, concluded with the statement "… research will continue." And it most certainly did.

Mr. Butcher was a keen amateur archaeologist and member of the Hunter Archaeological Society. He was inspired by the Council for British Archaeology's survey and Policy document (1948) and a statement that Bronze Age field systems and enclosed areas should be precisely surveyed and measured, not merely photographed or roughly mapped. He was trained in geology and as a mining surveyor; coming later to archaeology when he became intensely interested in understanding all aspects of landscape evolution from geological formations, soil development and the impact of man. This background and his enthusiasm led to him venturing onto the South Yorkshire/North Derbyshire moorlands where he discovered settlement sites that he recognised as being of Bronze Age. He set out to record all the earthworks pre the period of Parliamentary enclosure, but excluding hill forts, barrows and linear earthworks. He also located medieval sites there and was in the process of surveying those at the time of his death (1975).

Figure 9. Leslie Harry Butcher at Wharncliffe Crags, Summer 1957.

Over a period of some twenty years most of Butcher's leisure time was spent on this survey work, ably assisted by various members of the Hunter Archaeological Society. His copious field notes and drawings were placed in the Sheffield City Museum archives.

Several people have studied Butcher's papers, Pauline Beswick and Dariel Merrills combined to write briefly about the man and his discoveries of Romano-British settlements at Wharncliffe and Medieval sites in the Peak District. Graham Makepeace who worked with Butcher on some of his surveys and digs also concentrated on the Romano-British settlements in his paper of 1985. However, he does tell us that the Wharncliffe quern site, and I quote, "was one of the main sites in the north of England." He also states that most of the workings were found below the crags.

In 1988 Liz Wright whilst a member of the Department of Archaeology and Prehistory at Sheffield University made a study of quern production and distribution utilising Butcher's work. She undertook a lot of research herself and concluded that most of the stones must have left the Wharncliffe site as roughouts to be finished elsewhere. She poses a question concerning distribution, because generally querns do not appear on local sites. She also suggests quern manufacture may have continued at Wharncliffe until about the middle of the second century AD. All are points of interest that need further research.

A geophysical survey and trial trenching over part of the site in 1993, prior to the laying of a gas pipeline, failed to detect any further substantial evidence.

In the autumn of 1999 the Archaeological Investigation section of English Heritage undertook a detailed survey of this quern manufacturing site following a fire covering quite a large section of the northern part of the site in 1996. This fire destroyed much of the vegetation on Wharncliffe Heath exposing even more traces of quern workings than would have been visible to Butcher and Wright. A team of half a dozen took most of October and November to complete their task. Their comprehensive report drew no conclusions but serves to add support to the discoveries of Butcher and Wright. They even used one of Butcher's distribution maps in this report. Yes, they did discover more top and bottom quern stones. In excess of 2,300 quern "roughs" were recorded during this survey and each one was photographed and its position logged; but they had to agree with Wright's suggestion that querns were rarely completed on this site as there was no evidence of beehive querns with traces of hopper or feed hole, although a few flat disc type with central hole were unearthed.

Figure 10. One of the few disc stones with central hole that have been unearthed on the Wharncliffe site.

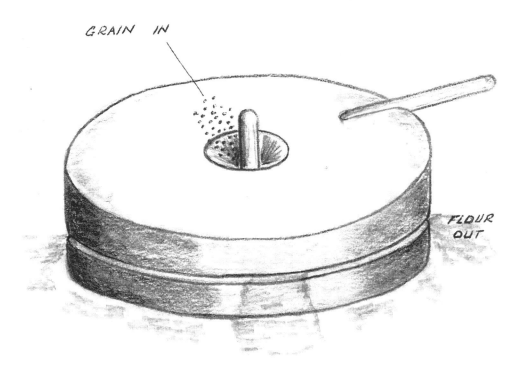

GRAIN IN

FLOUR OUT

Figure 11. This sketch of a rotary quern, displayed in Sheffield's Weston Park Museum, shows an upper stone of millstone grit which was excavated by the Hunter Archaeological Society in 1978 at Hopton in Derbyshire. A lower, flat disc of millstone grit found at Firth Park is also in the Museum.

Modern milling

Throughout the Roman occupation and indeed subsequently the population of Britain became more and more engaged in farming activities and the rotary quern had "caught on" with both farmers and settlers using them in the home.

The expanding Roman road network linked an ever increasing number of their forts. The legions within required substantial quantities of flour to feed them. They replaced hand grinding with much larger animal powered flour mills, oxen or horses and even slaves providing the power.

Figure 12. The Romans replaced hand grinding with much larger animal-powered flour mills

Watermills were probably introduced into Britain as long ago as the Roman times and certainly the Saxons used them in increasing numbers. More than 500 are recorded in the Domesday Survey of 1086, of which about eighty were in Derbyshire. One that appeared in the survey was the original Worsborough (Barnsley) Mill, although the present one dates from around 1625.

Later, man learned how to use wind power to drive mills. Windmills were built and became familiar features of the countryside.

Both watermills and windmills could generate sufficient power to drive stones much larger than quern stones, averaging 1.5 metres in diameter, 300mm. thick and weighing about 2 tonnes.

Figure 13. Unfinished millstones.

Butcher only found a few of this type of millstone on the Wharncliffe quern site; but many remain, in various stages of manufacture, on Hathersage Moor and Stanage Moor (see Figure 13). In 1900 there were an estimated 10,000 mills operating in the UK – 20 years later the number was below 2,000 – but they still used the traditional millstones just as they had hundreds of years ago.

The unreliability of wind and water and the ever increasing demand for flour combined to encourage some mill owners to convert to steam power. Their output still could not meet the demand. In fact farmers were unable to supply sufficient grain so Britain started to import wheat from Canada and America. As a result we now have large purpose built flour mills, mostly adjacent to ports. These mills utilise modern technology, grinding the wheat between steel rollers, driven by steam or electricity, to produce an extremely fine flour with no impurities.

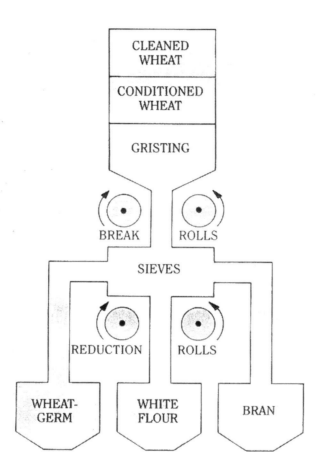

Figure 14. A simplified diagram of the modern milling process

In the past, wheat was ground between huge millstones in windmills. The flour that resulted was coarse. Today's flour is much finer because the process uses modern technology.

It is interesting to note that while the millstones wore down during the grinding process, small particles of the stone ended up in the flour. Many years of eating stone-ground flour in the form of bread and cakes etc. resulted in a lot of wear and tear on the teeth. Archaeological finds throughout the country have shown that skeletons of medieval date very often have teeth which are significantly worn down.

Modern milling processes pass the wheat through as many as twenty sets of steel rollers to obtain the finest of flours that are available today.

Illustrations

We acknowledge our thanks for permission to use the illustrations included in this monograph, as follows:

Frontispiece and Figures 12 and 14 - Flour Advisory Bureau
Figures 1 and 2 - Tom Tomlinson, Hathersage Parochial Church Council.
Figures 4, 5, 6, 7, 8, 9, 10 - Author's own material
Figure 13 - Reproduced from a "notelet" Viewpoints Images of England, Millstone Cards, Bakewell.

Bibliography

This bibliography lists the articles, books, leaflets and papers that have been most useful in the preparation of this monograph. The books have their own bibliographies, leading the interested to further reading.

English Heritage, *Quern Manufacturing at Wharncliffe* (Report, 2000)
Flour Advisory Bureau (Leaflets, 1998)
Mel Jones, *Making of the South Yorkshire Landscape* (Wharncliffe Books, 2000)
G.A. Makepeace, *Report on the Romano-British Settlement* (Hunter Archaeological Society Transactions; Vol. 13, 1985)
Chris Morley, *Grenoside* (Pamprint, 1996)
South Yorkshire County Council, *Worsborough Mill Museum* (Leaflet)
Tom D. Tomlinson, *Querns, Millstones and Grindstones* (Hathersage Parochial Church Council, 1981)
Philip Wilkinson, *What the Romans did for us* (Boxtree, 2000)
Liz Wright, *Beehive Quern Manufacture in the S.E. Pennines* (Scottish Archaeological Review, Vol. 5, 1988)

Also my thanks to the museums who co-operated.

The querns at Wharncliffe are best seen between late autumn, when the bracken and undergrowth have died back, and before its regrowth in spring.

UPDATE
Since this article was written part of the Wharncliffe quern factory has been designated as a Scheduled Monument (SY1253). ..."The extent and complexity of the Wharncliffe quern manufacturing site is unparalleled in the British Isles"....

Sheffield Wildlife Action Partnership (SWAP) recently commissioned ASE Ltd. (Archaeological Survey and Evaluation Limited) to carry out an archaeological survey of the Wharncliffe Heath Nature Reserve and its environs. This survey, undertaken in January 2003, discovered further evidence of quern manufacture, outside the limits of the Scheduled Monument site, but this had been included in Butcher's records.

3. File Cutting in Grenoside   *Philip Allison*

Files evidently originated in Egypt and have been used in Britain since the Bronze Age. They were traditionally made by hand, the teeth being cut with hammers and specially made chisels before the metal was hardened. This was a highly specialised and skilled hand process until the establishment of machine file making and cutting during the latter half of the nineteenth century.

There were a considerable number of hand file cutters in Grenoside. White's Directory of 1913 lists one file maker and six file cutters in Grenoside in that year and the last of these did not cease working until the late 1920s.

The date when file cutting was established in Grenoside is uncertain but a Directory of 1797 lists one filesmith in Ecclesfield and two in Grenoside.

White's Directory of 1841, lists three small firms of file manufacturers, noted as Naylor and Rhodes of Wharncliffe Works, also steel manufacturers; Joel Redfern file manufacturer and steel refiner and Benjamin Tingle, file and screw bolt manufacturer. Apart from Rhodes, these names are all listed in the 1841 census figures.

File manufacturing and file cutting in the nineteenth century were clearly important factors in the village economy. The numbers engaged in these occupations form a considerable percentage of the total workforce as shown by these figures:

	1841	**1861**
Total workforce	429	551
File cutters	82 = 19%	95 = 17%

The censuses do not give any indication as to whether or not the village file cutters were concerned as outworkers with the file blanks supplied from the Sheffield steel firms or blanks made locally in Grenoside steel works. It seems likely that the majority of the cutters would be working on blanks from outside the village especially during the latter part of the nineteenth century.

File cutting shop 1879

'The chief trade of the village is the cutting of files, the teeth of which are formed by a series of cuts made by a small chisel and hammer of peculiar construction. The sound of constant tapping thus made never fails to excite the curiosity of strangers to the mystery, especially in cold weather, when the otherwise open windows of the hulls, or small shops in which each family carries on the trade at home are closed by screens of oiled paper which let in sufficient light for a process which depends more upon the sense of touch than that of sight'.

The file blank was placed on a metal block let into the top of the stithy with the tang towards the cutter. The stithy was a heavy block of sandstone of some 6 1/4 cubic feet. The blank was held firm by a strap or stirrup which passed over the cutter's foot and over the file to anchorage points in the top of the stithy and the cutter could either clamp or release the file at will.

The faces of the blank would have been cleaned with various grades of file and lightly oiled. The tools for cutting were a hammer and chisel, both of special shapes specifically designed for this particular purpose. The distinctive feature of either of the seven pound or three pound hammers in use was the shaft which was angled at thirty degrees to the head to impart an angled cut to the blade face of the chisel and was also designed to be used with a flick of the wrist rather than a swing of the arm.

When the first side of the blank was completed a lead sheath was placed over the metal block of the stithy to protect the completed side whilst the second side was cut. The whole process was an extremely skilled craft for although the technique was basically simple it was performed with incredible rapidity. It seems remarkable that the necessary parallel cuts, sometimes as many as 100 to the inch for the finer files, could be made to the necessary accuracy at such speed as 60 blows per minute.

The contemporary print below shows a typical workshop.

The sketch below shows a typical file.

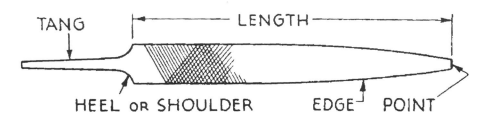

Each indentation required a shift of the chisel with one hand and a blow from the hammer in the other hand.

The amount of bodily force used in one day was considerable. A man would typically have worked 10 hours per day, striking 46,000 blows with a 3 kg hammer.

Like most of the trades available to Grenosiders in Victorian times the work could have appalling effect on health, as evidenced by the following statements made to an official enquiry in Sheffield in 1865.

George Bagnall, under manager of the file department at Messrs Ibbotson Bros. and Co., Russell Street,

'The lead used to cut the file upon and the dust which flies up make it unhealthy work; forging is a good deal healthier. Colic is a very nasty complaint amongst file cutters, and you scarcely ever see a file cutter with good teeth, that shows the effect. Their teeth generally begin going when they are about 18. Sitting and stooping too so much over the work, as is necessary, is bad for the chest.'

Charles Stark, file cutter in yard off Watery Lane,

'The right hand and wrist often become weak and waste, and get knots in the tendons. My right wrist is smaller than my left. Owing to the pressure of the chisel the left thumb is stunted and never grows properly, and also gets bent back, and is liable to have warts like this on the end, which are very painful.'

Such conditions which would be unthinkable today were a normal part of life at the time as reflected in the following extracts from works by contemporaries. The first a poem by J. Roebuck from his 'Collection of Poems'.

FILE CUTTERS
In memory of Joe Dawson, The Common (Ecclesfield)

Often when walking down the street, about nine in the morn,
A horny-handed man you'd meet, at waist an apron worn.
He was a member of the host of those who cut the files,
Seated all day at his stithy post, exchanging yarns 'tween whiles.

With foot in stirrup, file in block, with bended back and peering eyes,
And chisel held firm as a rock, see how his hammer flies.
He'd cut triangle, rounds or that, half round, and specials, too;
T'was marvellous at his stithy sat, what jobs this man could do.

Oft times you'd find a stithy block within a human dwelling;
A woman working at the stock, meanwhile the dough was swelling.
Wielding a hammer with such strength, to watch her was entrancing,
As down the cold files steely length she sent the chisel dancing.

Both sons and daughters, wives as well, they each one did their part
To make the weekly output swell, and load the carrier's cart
With forks and gimlets, rasps and files, all packed up nice and neat
Being carried from the shops, 'tween whiles, along the village street.

Each file was blacked after 'twas cut, then wrapped in paper brown;
Into their bundle they were put and carried into town
Where they were hardened off at last, as hard as aught could be,
A file that really would outlast the use of you and me.

The second extract is from Harold Wasteney's "Grenoside Recollections"

The file cutters, of which there were quite a number, had their own workshops and were a class apart; they worked when they liked and "laiked" also. Some used their own houses, the front room was the favourite and the family were taught this trade as early as seven years of age. The girls would cut the smaller files, as great patience was needed to do the very tedious and exacting work. The file cutter was paid, like the baker, at the rate of thirteen to the dozen, which meant he would have to cut a file for nothing before earning anything for himself.

He never appeared in the early part of the week to commence work. Receiving his batch of blank files on the Saturday, they would lay till Monday. If he worked in his own shop, or with a colleague, he would turn up at the shop in a clean white apron about nine o'clock, take it off, put it on the crutch (seat) on which he worked, look about him, then at the window and, uncertain of what to do next, walk up and down. He would then stop and examine his petty cash, which would not be much after the weekend roistering, and, having made a decision, quickly leave the shop, deciding that was that for the day.

This decision may have been prompted by the thought that there was a meeting of the beagles, some rabbit coursing or perhaps trap-pigeon shooting, he not being the type to miss what was going if it was a diversion. Failing this, there was always the solace of a pint.

Arriving at the shop on Tuesday he would don his apron, take the blank files and begin to strip them, that is to file off any sharp edges to facilitate the easy movement of the chisel when cutting. Finishing this job he would then see to the lead pads. They being to his satisfaction, an inspection of the chisels would be required. Some would require sharpening on the grindstone, which most shops possessed, together with a hand bellows, furnace and an anvil. Should the chisel have become too blunt it would be treated by the fire, drawn out on the anvil and afterwards tempered.

The grinding wheel was a ponderous heavy wheel and required some effort to spin at the necessary speed. Having done this, he would leap smartly on to the seat and endeavour to sharpen the chisel to his satisfaction before the wheel ceased to revolve. The oil in the pot would be inspected and filled up if required (a smear of this oil was put on each file face to facilitate easy chipping of the chisel when cutting). All this would have now taken him up to about twelve o'clock and feeling the need for some like company he would put up the shutters and that was that for another day. It will be noted he had not yet earned a copper.

Wednesday sees him at the shop a little earlier and, commencing work with not too much enthusiasm, is quick to cease should an acquaintance drop in, especially if he should have the "Early Bird" (a sporting paper) and point out a "known cert" in the afternoon race card. This would lead to lengthy discussions on the horses' merits and chances of victory, during which time no files were being cut. About four thirty or so, after working half-heartedly, he would decide to call that another day. Thursday morning dawned and, realising what he had not done, he would make a very early start. Looking at the heap of uncut files made him realise that there would be "nowt" to draw at the weekend so he worked like a demon, no time for dinner, hastily swallowed tea and back to the shop until midnight. The same again on Friday, finishing cutting and having the files bundled in time for the carrier to collect.

Not all carried on like his; the more thrifty types spread the work throughout the week and some, rather than pay the carrier's fee, would carry their work to the firm in Sheffield and return with the following week's work.

It could be said it was not a healthy occupation; stooping over their work, together with the lead dust they must inhale, was no inducement to long life. The day of the hand file cutter was challenged by the machine, which was able to produce files faster and more cheaply, but the diehards would vow and declare that no machine-cut file could equal the hand-cut. This could be a case of sour grapes, as the file using industry was well satisfied with the machine-cut product. So another industry in the village ceased; the last file cutter died in 1928.

These very substantial stithies or work benches are virtually all that remains of a file cutter's workshop. The iron plates (called anvils or stocks) to which the file and lead sheet were strapped can be clearly seen.

Both the writers of those pieces were witnesses of the file makers' trade and it is likely that a fair picture of what the average file maker was like lies somewhere between Mr Roebuck's rosy picture and Mr Wasteney's more acerbic view.

We must be glad that no one here today has to labour for so long, for so little, under such unhealthy conditions at such tedious work. That such men, women and even children survived to produce later generations of honest, upright folk must be a matter of pride for the village.

Sources

Census records for Grenoside, 1841 and 1861.

J. Roebuck, *Collection of Poems.*

H. Wasteney, *Grenoside Recollections.*

White's Directory, 1841 and 1913.

Acknowledgement

Permission to quote from Harold Wasteney's "Grenoside Recollections" was given by his daughter, Mrs Doreen Wilson.

4. Nailmaking   *Lyn Howsam*

Bronze nails are known to have been used by the Celts but it was with the arrival of the Romans in Britain that nails made of iron became more widely used. As the Roman troops moved around Britain the nails were used in the construction of forts and other buildings. When the time came for the troops to move on, the buildings were taken down and the nails carefully extracted for future use. During the Middle Ages there was an increase in the demand for nails as they were used for many other things such as shoe and boot making.

One of the main occupations in the parish of Ecclesfield and its surrounding areas including Grenoside, during the 17th and 18th century and probably earlier, was that of nailmaking. Indeed in his will of 1506, John Hill is described as a nailor and Thomas Cutts of Ecclesfield was also referred to, as a nailmaker in his will of 1583. Memories of the trade are few and those that remain speak of the distressed nailor, uncouth and poverty-stricken, an object of contempt or pity living in depressed conditions in the 19th century. But in an earlier age of nailmaking, the average nailor had an adequate standard of living while the middlemen of the trade were of the same social and economic standing as Yeomen. It was a seasonal occupation often combined with that of farming. A Wortley clerk explained to a London agent in 1747 that he had been able to send only 52 bags of nails because `the naylors are busy with the harvest.' From March to August nails would be made for the London market. At Harvest time the nailors would be too busy to make nails until the autumn when flat pointed nails would be made for export to Virginia. For the West Indies, sharp points would be made after Martinmas (Nov 11th) until it was time to prepare the soil yet again. In 'An Old Ecclesfield Diary' there are a list of Nail Shops in Ecclesfield giving names and number of hearths each person had. Written at the bottom is '42 Harths at (4 per hearth) = 168 pair of hands'. There is no indication where the list came from or for what purpose it was compiled. In many other nailmaking areas of the country it was usual for the women and children to be involved in the trade. But in Ecclesfield, Grenoside and other areas local to these there is no evidence to support this, certainly with regard to the women. The trade did quite often involve several members of the same family working in their own smithy.

A look at the 19th century censuses for Grenoside shows us the main families involved in nailmaking. It can be seen also from the same censuses the decline in the trade although these figures may be slightly unreliable due to boundary changes that occurred when each census was taken. –

38 Nailmakers in the village in 1841. Addys, Ashton, Battys, Bowers, Fosters, Hagues, Hobsons, Horsefields, Houselys, Kay, Kirk, Marsden, Senior, Unwin, Tingle and Wilsons.

22 in 1851. Addy, Allotts, Andrews, Armison, Beard, Bower, Fosters, Hagues, Hobsons, Houseley, Jamison, Kays and Wilson.

Only 8 in 1861. Allott, Bower, Dales, Foster, Gill, Unwin & Wilson.

9 in 1871. Allott, Bowers, Dales, Foster, Kays. (3 of whom were aged over 70 years)

And just 2 in 1881. Brothers George and Robert Dale. John Allott had turned to making Rivets.

By the 1891 census the trade had died out completely in the village.

The youngest person to be found working at the trade was 12 year old Benjamin Kay in the 1851 Census. This I'm sure does not reflect the true number who 'helped out' at various times within the family smithy. The oldest nailmaker still working was 80 year old Joseph Wilson in the 1861 census.

Albert Goddard in his book "Yesterday in Grenoside" talks of a few in the village 'who were very old' when he was just a small boy. (Albert was born in 1880). He refers to George Dale, nail maker and rate collector who lived on Woodside Lane and author of 'Methodism in the village of Grenoside', sincere and just, who gave his life to the Saviour, and followed "In His Steps". George would probably have been around 45 at the time Albert is probably talking about. Some areas of the country did continue the trade well into the 20th century. In the Black Country one lady remembers her grandmother as late as 1904 still working as a nailmaker. In Hoylandswaine, another local nailmaking area, it is thought that the Chappell family's hearth was being used as late as 1940 when a small pickup truck from David Brown's Foundry at Penistone was sent to pick up a consignment of hand made nails from the Hoylandswaine Nail Shop.

A typical nailmaker's smithy

The craft was easy to learn and required very little capital to set up. The work was carried out in a smithy, which was either an off-shot building attached to the house or a simple workshop in the backyard. All that was needed was a hearth, an anvil, and a few tools such as a hammer, vices and bellows and of course the rod iron and coke. The basic process was to heat the rods of iron in a coke fire, which was kept hot by means of hand bellows and then to cut the iron to the required length over a 'cold sate' let into the anvil with the cutting edge upwards. The rod iron was then placed in a hole in the anvil and given a sharp tap with a hammer to form a head. This caused the nail to jump out of the hole leaving it vacant for the next. All this was done at incredible speed. It is said that a craftsman required just 12 strikes of the hammer to finish one nail - taking just 6 seconds to complete. The rod iron had to be of very good quality to enable the nails to penetrate the hard English oak. Local ironstone was used and there was sufficient for their needs at the slitting mill at Wortley. This was powered by water to work the hammers that cut the iron into bars and then into rods. Deliveries of the rod iron from the Wortley Slitting Mill to areas like Mortomley would be made in the 'iron wayne', a wagon pulled by two horses. The iron wayne was first heard of in 1647 and, according to local legend, was still going strong in 1908 although 'the original wheels had worn out to be replaced by new, then a new body was later fitted and then new wheels again' and so on throughout the centuries! Some nailers would collect their own rod iron while delivering their nails to the nail chapmen. The first slitting mill is known to have opened in Kent as early as 1590.

As Ecclesfield was the recognised centre of the trade for South Yorkshire during the 18th century, it was here that the nailers of several townships met to sign an agreement aimed at enforcing the apprenticeship regulations. As more and more men were taking up the trade and many more nails were being produced this resulted in a reduced income. The nailmakers did not like this at all and in 1733 a nail Chapman called Jonathan Deardon, along with 12 other nail chapmen in the area was responsible for the drawing up of the Nailmakers Agreement. The main purpose of this agreement was to ensure that apprentices served a full 7 years apprenticeship. Previously they had only served two years after which time -
'Apprentices so taken do follow the business and act as masters themselves and do marry very young and inconsiderately and by that means do have a great charge of children to maintain before they scarce know how to maintain themselves.'

The agreement intended not only to prevent early marriages but also to keep down the number of nailmakers setting up in business. Over two hundred nailmakers from the surrounding areas of Sheffield, Rotherham, Barnsley, Wath, Grenoside, Thorpe Hesley & Chapeltown etc. signed the agreement. Of these 94 could actually sign their names - the others made their mark. Those who did sign the document were the hearthmasters themselves so it is obvious that there were many more people who worked alongside them actually involved in the trade at the time.

In 1739, William Spencer of Cannon Hall, proposed to manufacture nails for the London market as well as the export trade. He employed Jonathan Deardon as his taker in of nails as Deardon's standing in the trade had already been demonstrated by his name at the head of organisers of the Ecclesfield Nailmakers Agreement. The nailors appear to have been under contract to work for Spencer either as outworkers in their own smithies or under Deardon's direct supervision at Howbrook. Deardon paid the outworkers either at Howbrook or their local warehouse at stated times. He was responsible for overseeing the transporting of the nails to the inland port of Bawtry where they would then be sent on to various places all over the world. In a letter to Deardon, Spencer referred to 'all the rod iron in your warehouses.' These warehouses appear to have belonged to Deardon, as they never feature in Spencer's accounts. Like other chapmen, Deardon had sufficient resources to be able to allow the nailors credit. Not long after this the nailmakers in the area ran into difficulties when they were being undersold by the nailmakers of Birmingham. The chapmen urged the ironmasters to reduce the price of rod iron, which they did with great reluctance but this failed to improve things. The nailmakers themselves were also to blame for a drop in the trade due to substandard work.

In 1742 there were problems with faulty nails being sent to London and there were angry exchanges of letters between Deardon and Spencer's clerk in London, William Murgatroyd. He complained of the poor quality of the nails he had received - 'A great many of them having no heads and some without points and some having neither.' Deardon claimed this was due to the bad iron that Spencer had supplied him with but Spencer's reply was that all nails should have a good head and point on them be the iron good or bad. Deardon visited London to see for himself and there was an agreement to go to arbitration at a cost of £1000 each. Before this could be done, Spencer angrily sacked Deardon and closed down his operation and in October 1742 Spencer wrote 'I have now discontinued the nail trade and discharged Jonathan Deardon so a great number of naylors are at present unemployed.' This was only a temporary setback and the trade continued to flourish into the next century when the machine made nails from America and France flooded the market. It was largely replaced by other crafts or by the new iron works or coalmines such as Newton Chambers at Thorncliffe. America had begun to make their own nails after the War of Independence in 1775 - the first nail cutting machine being brought into use in 1811 and continuing to improve during the 19c. Orders from the Navy had also ceased with the end of the Wars with France. It was much the same all over the main nailmaking areas such as the Midlands and Belper.

The Nailmakers Agreement originally kept in the parish chest at St Mary's Ecclesfield is now safely deposited in the Sheffield City Archives and is on parchment 32 inches x 27. The names are in 9 columns each with a red seal between the Christian name and surname. Unfortunately it does not give the place of residence of those who signed the document though many are recognizable as being local surnames. One of the names on the agreement is of a Samuel Walker - possibly the Samuel Walker who was born at Grenoside to Joseph Walker and Ann Hargreaves in 1715. Joseph Walker was a nailmaker of Grenoside having lived at Hollins House and at the time of drawing up his will 'of Stubbing House'. The inventory of his possessions drawn up by his friends at the time of his death in 1729 totaling £61-6-8 shows that he was a man of moderate means. One son Jonathan concentrated on farming while Aaron followed the dual occupation of his father, farming and nailmaking. Samuel however became a schoolmaster but like most others at the time would still have needed to supplement his income. His interest with nailmaking continued and he had a smithy at the back of his house in which he continued to work experimenting with various processes. Eventually he was to build a foundry at Masbro. David Hey in his article 'The Nailmaking Backgrounds of The Walkers & The Booths' states 'Nailmaking helped to found the base on which the Industrial Revolution was forged. From the ranks of the nailmakers came the new ironmasters; and when the population explosion of the eighteenth century created a labour force for the new works, the mass of people in South Yorkshire were already used to industrial activity through their involvement in nailmaking and other secondary iron trades.'

A report in the Sheffield Iris in 1795 tells of an argument between two brothers who were both nail makers working in the same forge in Ecclesfield. During their disagreement one brother on sudden impulse ran the red-hot end of a bar of iron, which he had just removed from the fire, into the belly of his brother. 'The flesh closed upon the iron which, in the midst of the agonies of the poor man, was with much difficulty extracted. He languished a while in torment and then expired. The more unfortunate wretch who survives is to take his trial at the York Assizes.'

Sources

C. Reg. Andrews, *The Story of Wortley Ironworks*

The Nailmakers Agreement: Transcription by R. Butterworth, Hunter Archaeological Society Vol. II (1924) pages 114-119.

Cynthia Dalton, *Nailmaking in Hoylandswaine*

David Hey, *The Nailmaking Background of the Walkers and the Booths*

David Hey, *The Village of Ecclesfield* (Huddersfield, 1968).

David Hey, *The Rural Metalworkers of the Sheffield Region* (Leicester, 1972).

Sheffield Iris 1795 - Newspaper collection of Sheffield Local Studies Library.

Thomas Winder, ed., *An Old Ecclesfield Diary* (1921).

5. Gannister Mining *David Diver*

Grenoside stands on a series of sedimentary rocks deposited by a great river forming a delta in the sea some 300,000,000 years ago. The sediments were the result of frost, ice and rain wearing down a huge range of mountains in what is now called Scotland.

Over millions of years the material suspended in the river(s) changed, with the result that differing layers were deposited as Millstone Grit, Mudstones, Silts, Coal, Gannister and others to a depth of about 4,400 feet.

FEET

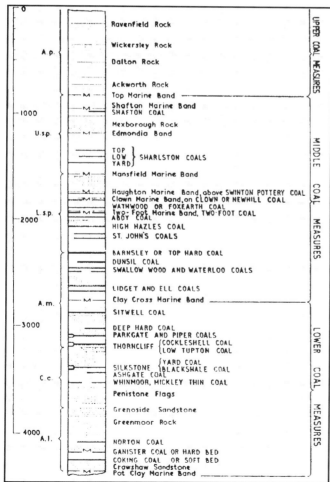

This took about 60,000,000 years, and included 80-100 coal seams.

Generalized section of the Coal Measures, showing the chief marine bands, coal seams and sandstones.
IPR/38-27C British Geological Survey
© *NERC All rights reserved.*

39

More easily appreciated is the following diagram which illustrates the various layers that concern us here.

Typical cycles of deltaic sediments from the British coal measures

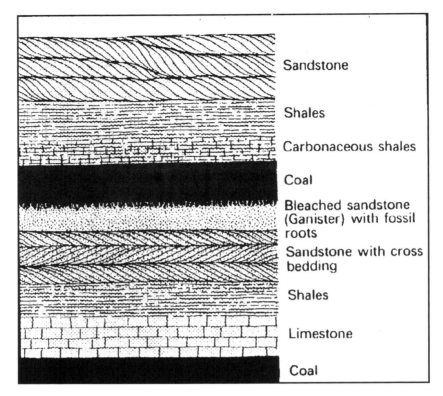

Some idea of the countless layers of sandstone beneath our feet is given by this photograph.

Today, the horizontal beds shown above have been tilted and fractured by movements of the Earth's crust, and ice, water, wind and frost have made great changes in the surface creating the topography in the cross-section below.

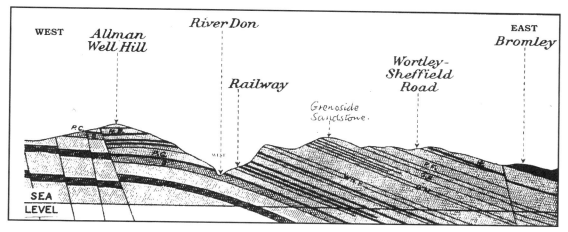

The rock on which our village stands - "The Grenoside Sandstone" (GR on the cross-section) - is present over a wide area which stretches as far as Halifax and has been used as building stone and for various other purposes for thousands of years.

From the section you will see that to the west of the Grenoside Sandstones, as the hill drops down to the Don, a number of different layers are exposed. Among these are several seams of coal coming to the surface in a way which made it possible to extract by means of drift mines, where tunnels were dug into the hillside and the thin seams of coal were followed down the gentle underground slope. It seems likely that coal had been extracted here for many years before large scale mining began, but it was probably only used for local domestic heating, lacking as it did both quality and quantity.

If you walk through Beeley Wood, or the lower part of Wharncliffe Woods, you will find extensive signs of mining, now obscured by decades of undergrowth. If it wasn't coal, what were they mining? The answer is gannister - a fine grained sandstone of great purity which when crushed and then ground on a machine like this - produced a powder which was

moistened to form a clay from which furnace bricks or moulded linings and fittings were made for the booming steel trade. The trade flourished from the mid 1800s and did not end until the 1940s.

Gannister resulted from the regular cycle of the seabed sinking under the weight of the old deposits and new layers being deposited by the river(s). Then great forests sprang up on the new land. These forests eventually died and rotted down then sank into the sea and were duly crushed to form coal. These forests were rooted in a bed of sand from which the plants extracted everything but the quartz grains which then, when cemented together with siliceous material, were compressed into Gannister.

Gannister was important because firstly it was capable of withstanding the extremely high temperatures being used by the latest steel production methods and secondly because of its high purity. The toughness of this particular rock had been noted much earlier when it was used as a material for making roads. By no means a rare mineral, geological accident placed vast quantities in our backyard in easily accessible places and so the upper Don Valley became well known in the steel industry with "Beeley Blue Best" as its star product.

Though easily accessible the rock was extremely hard to work - much harder than ordinary sandstone. Doug Sanderson of Oughtibridge knows more than most about the life of the miners and has given me permission to quote from his article in "Look Local" 25 April 2002.

What was life like for the gannister miner?

"Very often he was obliged to become a miner because there was no other work available. If he was lucky enough to get employment at an open cast quarry site, the conditions were not too bad, but work in the drift mines was often dangerous and unpleasant. Frequently, the drifts would be running in water and he would be lying on his back or side, picking at the work face or filling the trucks or 'corves', as they were known, ready for them to be pulled out of the mine on the miniature railway, by one of the ponies kept for the purpose. Ventilation shafts provided a certain amount of fresh air and helped to prevent the build up of gas. Even so, the atmosphere was often thick with silica dust resulting from the use of dynamite, and from the tools in constant contact with the rock.

The miner would begin his day by dressing in a fashion that was almost a uniform for all the gannister miners. A thick shirt, open at the neck, into which was tucked a brightly coloured handkerchief, and sleeves rolled up above the elbows. Corduroy trousers would be held up by braces and a leather belt and tied with string below the knee as a safety precaution, or perhaps to prevent one of the many rats from entering. Clogs were the footwear of the day as they were the only shoes that could stand the harsh conditions. His attire was completed with a cloth cap similar to those worn by all the working class of the day, and a waistcoat. Work began by collecting candles from the pit office, that were to be his only means of illumination in the pit, before the introduction of lamps. They also served to indicate how many hours he had been underground and when his shift was over. He would arrive home covered in dirt to find a large zinc bathtub in front of the kitchen fire and his wife busy filling it with jugs of hot water from the Yorkshire Range, ready for him to have a bath. Such was the hard life of the gannister miner.

Away from the pit he could be found enjoying his sport, playing Knur and Spell, Hound Trailing or attending the local chapel with his wife and family. Their reward was often a life in miserable housing conditions, with a single fire providing heat obtained from what coal he could manage to bring home from the mine."

I find it fascinating that if you stand on Jawbone Hill and look down towards Oughtibridge much of the land you can see is honeycombed with mine tunnels. The same applies to the other side of the valley to Worrall and on the nearside along to Deepcar.

Looking west from where the Birley Stone has stood for nine hundred years or more, it is hard to believe that beneath this pastoral scene lies a maze of tunnels.

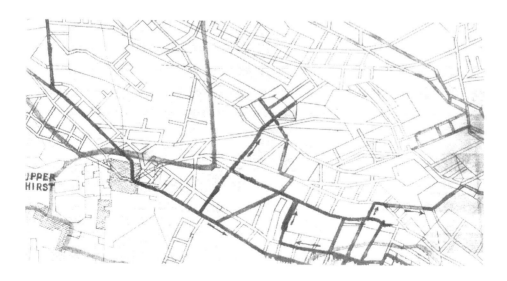

This reduced drawing is taken from a larger linen map covering the land visible from Jawbone Hill. The area shown is about 320 metres x 180 metres. Nothing on the surface to be seen from Jawbone gives any clue that beneath the agricultural scene below lies this complex of tunnels. The dark lines indicate the direction of air flows. This extract shows less than a tenth of the full drawing which (I can only guess) covers perhaps a third of the area on the east side of the Don nearest to Grenoside from which gannister was extracted. However sketchy this information may be, there can be no doubt that here was a significant industry.

Another clue to the extent of the working is the following extract from the "Early History of Stocksbridge".

"In 1908, the output of gannister in the West Riding of Yorkshire alone was 80,124 tons, of which fully one half was raised in our valley, our estimate for that year being about 40,000 tons, for all the collieries situated below Underbank Reservoir, including the extensive working under Wharncliffe Wood."

A group taken in 1902 at the Old Ganister Pit, Stocksbridge.
Original photo kindly loaned by Mr. L. Travis, Spink Hall Estate, Stocksbridge)

The miners portrayed had hard and often short lives. Their working methods are illustrated by this extract from "Science and art of Mining" Nov. 4, 1905.

"In working the gannister, post and stall, or double stall has been found the best and most economical method of working, owing to the unevenness of the floor, the large quantity of packing material required, and the distance between the last pack and the face when the gannister has been bared ready for blasting. The gannister, of course, is bared by working away the coal, either for long or short distances, according to the demand for either mineral. Two men and a boy generally work together; the men do the blasting and the boy the tramming. The holes are drilled by hand, as no machine drill, except one driven by mechanical power, would face the hard substance which is sometimes drilled through, although the floor generally, is fire clay. Owing to the inconvenience of the floor, only experienced men are able to drill the holes to any useful depth, which varies according to the quantity of work to be done. As much as three pounds of dynamite has often been used to blow a thickness of about three feet in a narrow place, or there are what are known as "roots," and occasionally, in very bad places, the miner will use the whole box of dynamite - five pounds - without blowing a single "corf" of the mineral. These "roots" are not the ordinary rootlets which we collect as fossils, but depressions in the floor similar to channels, the gannister sometimes running from two feet to six feet thick in a space of two or three yards ... In mining this mineral large quantities of dust are raised by the blasting operations which have to be resorted to, and also in the crushing and grinding departments on the surface. This dust is very injurious if breathed to any extent as it gets on the lungs and cannot be dislodged, consequently, anyone

working in it sooner or later becomes a victim to what is known as "gannister disease" or "miners' phthisis", a kind of consumption which takes hold of the unfortunate fellow, who eventually succumbs to it when he still ought to be in the prime of life. .. "

Drilling under ganister in clay with hand-drill, for a charge of dynamite.

Nothing remains now except some strange hollows in the hillside, a few tracks, an inclined plane, a factory still producing refractory products (but not from gannister) and the odd broken brick structure.

Where once you might have heard the boom of the miners' dynamite, or the clink of his pick on the rock, the neigh of his pony as it dragged the loaded cove out of the mine, now you will only hear the distant noise of the traffic groaning its way up the hill or the excited barking of my dog as it chases squirrels through the woods.

While it is disappointing that we have so little record of a century of back-breaking, lung tearing work, so vital to the steel industry, perhaps it is best that the ugly signs of their labour are now hidden in dense afforestation. An industry gone and sadly almost forgotten.

6. Killed by a Bear - in the Parish of Ecclesfield!   *Lyn Howsam*

Among some of the sports popular in Grenoside were those of rabbit coursing, live pigeon shooting and on Lump Green in the 1800's, bull, bear and badger baiting are known to have taken place. A house on Lump Lane, now long since demolished was known as the Bear House and it was here that the bear was kept for the sport. These activities were common in many places at that time. In Revd. J. Eastwood's `History of the Parish of Ecclesfield' 1862, it is said that 'Bear baiting was carried out on the open space on the south-west corner of the churchyard where still stands a stout post which has been pointed out as the bull and bear stake.' Revd. Gatty also wrote of the brutal sports that were popular at feasts and local fairs. 'Within living memory there were periodical bull and bear baiting for which a bull and two bears were kept.'

The poor animal would be tied to the post and set upon by fierce savage dogs specially kept for this purpose. The dog would attempt to pin the animal to the floor by its snout while the crowd yelled its approval. The blood and cries of pain from the animal were considered to be entertaining along with the gambling and drinking that accompanied it. These animals were specially bred to kill. Cock fighting was another common sport and the claws, beaks and teeth would be specially sharpened and spurs fitted to inflict the greatest possible injury. There was lots of rivalry between the villages to breed the best and again drinking and gambling would take place. It was not unknown when things were too quiet for workers, for them to seek out stray animals, tie them to a post and stone them to death. From time to time accidents and deaths would result from such dangerous sports and one in particular that occurred at High Green in the parish of Ecclesfield is well documented.

Francis Rodger was born in 1751 at Wadsley, the eldest of seven sons and one daughter born to Richard and Mary Rodger and baptised at St Mary's Ecclesfield. The family had moved to Thomson Hill (sic), at High Green shortly after Francis's birth and like many inhabitants in the area were mainly nailmakers. In 1772 at the age of 21 Francis married Ann Woodcock from the neighbouring parish of Tankersley at St Mary's church Ecclesfield. The couple was blessed with 5 children - Esther, Martha, Joseph, Judith, and Sarah. In 1782 when Sarah the youngest was six months old, Ann aged just 31 years old died and was buried in St Mary's graveyard. Francis like many men in those days finding themselves widowed with young children to look after married again just 14 months later. It was in Jan 1784 when Mary Askew aged 21 years, daughter of John and Mary Askew of White Lane Chapeltown, became the second wife of Francis Rodger aged 33. The couple was destined to have just over 6 years together before Mary met her death in a tragic and terrible way. During those 6 years the couple had four children, Pheby, Charles, Mary, who died before she could be baptised, and lastly Lydia born in August 1790. Just four months after Lydia's birth, Mary, aged 29yrs tragically lost her life leaving her young family motherless. It was a brief entry in 'An Old Ecclesfield Diary' that first drew my attention to the terrible end to Mary's life:

'1790 Mary wife of Frans. Rodger she was bitten by Wm Cooper's bear at High Green Dec 11. She died of her wounds the Munday (sic) following Dec 13.'

The diary had been kept it is believed by one Septimus Lister, an inhabitant of Ecclesfield parish and covers the years between 1775-1845 in which he recorded some of the day-to-day goings on in the area. The diary was edited by Thomas Winder and published in 1921. The entry gives no clue as to how the incident had occurred nor was there any mention of anyone else being hurt. Nor does it say whether the bear had broken loose when being baited. There would of course have been no death certificate issued, as Civil Registration did not begin until 1837. So what was the true story? Fortunately, despite High Green being a small hamlet just seven miles away from Sheffield at the time, a report of the incident was published in the local newspaper:

Sheffield Register Dec 1790
'A circumstance not less dreadful in its consequence, than disgraceful to a civilized nation, happened at High Green, a few miles from hence, on Saturday morning last. A bear kept there by one Cooper, for the amusement of the country people at their wakes, got loose - pinched it is for food - and entered the dwelling of a person named Rogers. The unfortunate wife of the man was sitting with one child on her lap and another beside her, when the creature seized her with all the savage ferocity incident to it's nature, and tore her in a manner too shocking to particularize. The cries of the poor unfortunate, and of the children, reached Rogers and the Bearward, who almost at the same moment entered the house, and beheld a sight sufficient to appal the most callous mind - what then must have been the feelings of the husband? - He flew to the animal, but was unable to wrench its jaws from the object of its fury. Cooper then struck it on the head with a hammer, but the haft flying off, the blow was powerless; it however turned the bent of its rage on him, and it pursued him until he was nearly exhausted with fatigue, and he must have fallen a victim, had not the neighbours, alarmed at the outcries, come up with him, and, at a second shot, laid it dead. - The woman expired in dreadful agony on Monday. We hope and trust this dreadful and unparalleled accident will finally abolish, in these parts, that unchristian, barbarous species of diversion - bear-baiting.' (sic)

Her death must have been extremely painful and distressing, also very traumatic for the family. Sadly Mary's burial is wrongly recorded in the parish register on the 15th Dec 1790 as 'Sarah' wife of Francis Rodger.

Francis, now with 8 children to look after, had no choice but to marry again and just 8 months later in Aug 1791 he married Elizabeth Kay. He was now 40 years old. The couple had 3 children Amelia 1792, Rueben 1794 and Niny 1798 making a total of 12 children that Francis had fathered. Apart from baby Mary, only Joseph born to Francis's first wife died young aged just 16 years. Francis died in 1810 aged 59 years. I do hope that the last years of his life were happy and free from further tragedy and heartache. I would very much like to think they were.

Francis and Mary Rodger are my great, great, great, great grandparents.

(A similar article by the author appeared in the Family Tree Magazine, July 2000.)

Sources

Revd. J. Eastwood, *A History of the Parish of Ecclesfield* (London, 1862).

Revd. A. Gatty, *A Life at One Living* (London, 1884).

David Hey, *The Village of Ecclesfield* (Huddersfield, 1968).

Parish Records of St Mary's, Ecclesfield – Sheffield City Archives.

Sheffield Register 1790 – Newspaper collection of Sheffield Local Studies Library.

Thomas Winder, ed., *An Old Ecclesfield Diary* (1921).

7. Grenoside Man Hanged at York *Lyn Howsam*

Entries from an 'Old Ecclesfield Diary' 1819

'Sunday morning about 3 'o'clock, *Sept.10th, Samuel Booth, Garrott, Ben Bower and J Bower, all armed With Gunns was met upon Warncliffe Moor By Mr Wortley's Stuards or Game Tenters Thos. Parkin & Joseph Parkin. Samuel Booth shot Thom. Parkin In to the Left Side & Thos. Parkin Fell to the Ground. The other 3 Set to Beating Joseph Parkin with the Butt of the Gunn Thos, Parkin Died of his Wounds Soon after, The Coroner Inquests Jury Brought in there Verditis against S. Booth, Garrott and John & Benj. Bower Who was Comited to York Castle and Take there Trials the Next Lent Assises
For the County of York 1820.' [sic]

******

*Although the diary gives Sept 10th as the date of this event, it would appear that it has been wrongly transcribed and should read Oct 10th. The event took place 9th/10th Oct. A few months later the following piece appears in the Diary

'Saml. Booth of Grenoside Exicuted at York for Shooting Thom. Parkin upon Wharncliffe Moore October 9th 1819. Exicuted March 13 1820' [sic]

******

Thomas and Joseph Parkin were both Gamekeepers employed in the service of James Archibald Stuart Wortley, Esq to look after his estate at Wharncliffe. Thomas was shot and later died on the Sunday night of Oct 10th while on the lookout for poachers. A Jury at a Coroners inquest brought in a verdict of *Wilful murder* after hearing evidence against the perpetrators of the crime - Samuel Booth, William Garrott and two brothers Benjamin and John Bower all residing in the village of Grenoside. The four men stood trial for the offence at the York Assizes in March 1820 and were charged with the murder of Thomas Parkin by shooting him through the body. Mr Cross stated the case for the prosecution and called on Joseph Parkin as the chief witness. Joseph told how he and Thomas had gone out on the night of the 10th October 1819 to look for poachers. About 4 o'clock they saw four men coming up the road towards them and he suggested to Thomas Parkin that they get out of sight. Before they could do that William Garrott had spotted them and ran towards them with the other three men following closely behind him. When Garrott came upon them Thomas had put his hand on Garrott's shoulder saying 'What my lad, is it you?'

They then carried on past the Bower brothers saying nothing to them but seeing the fourth man who was just a yard or two further away had a gun. Thomas Parkin went up to him and putting his hand on the outside of the man's pocket said. 'What, Sam thou hast got a gun I see: thou hast got a pocketful of snickles.' To which Booth replied, 'Damn thy soul, thou are going to rob me.' He turned round and pointing the gun at Thomas Parkin immediately shot him Thomas fell to the ground crying out that he had been shot. The moment he fell one of the other men seized Joseph Parkin while Booth struck him about the head and shoulder with the butt end of the gun. Joseph felt many other blows but could not say with certainty who struck those but he did recall John Bower's voice saying, 'Hit him. Hit him' or 'Stick him. Stick Him'. At that moment he heard a gun go off and managed to free himself and run off for assistance. It would appear from the evidence that Thomas Parkin, though badly injured, had managed at this moment to fire his gun, which wounded one of the attackers who then fell to the ground. The other three men fled the scene. When Joseph returned to the scene he found all four men had gone as had Thomas Parkin. Searching for him he later found him in a cottage near the roadside. The following evening Thomas died, a shot having gone through his left side and out the back. One of the accused men who had been shot by the first keeper was later found in bed at his own house recovering from his wounds. The accused all resided in the neighbouring village of Grenoside and though the others had all absconded they were later apprehended to stand trial. On Cross-examination Joseph Parkin stated that prior to the shot being fired there had been no assault committed on the prisoners either by himself or the deceased. A statement made by the deceased just prior to his death in the knowledge that his death was imminent was then read out in court. This statement agreed in every way with evidence of Joseph Parkin and expressly denied that there had been any preceding struggle with the four men involved.

Mr Hounsfield, surgeon of Sheffield, stated that the shot was the cause of the death. Dr Young and Mr Hounsfield both swore that the statement made by the deceased, was made knowing that death was inevitable. Other witnesses were examined, but their evidence was not thought to be relevant. The Constable involved in the case stated that Booth had alleged that the gun had gone off by accident.

Both Mr Coultman and Mr Jones, on the part of Wm. Garrett and Benj. Bower, contended that the firing of the gun by Bower was not in pursuance of any common object, in which they were jointly engaged; and therefore that they were not answerable for the acts of Booth. His Lordship said that was a consideration of the jury. No witnesses were called on the part of the prisoners.

His Lordship said, if the jury were satisfied of the fact that the deceased, being wilfully shot by the prisoner Booth, the jury were to consider whether the other prisoners were involved in the same transaction, and if so had gone out determined to join in any resistance that might be offered to their plans. If so, they would be equally guilty with the man who actually shot the deceased. The Jury, without retiring, found all the prisoners - Guilty. His lordship immediately passed sentence of death upon the prisoners, who were 'to be severally hung' the following Monday.

The Sheffield Mercury in its reporting of the case stated the following-
'We are to learn, that Mr Wortley, with characteristic humanity, made the most earnest intercession for the three younger, and that he happily succeeded in obtaining a reprieve for them. On Monday noon, the sentence of law was executed on Samuel Booth. The unfortunate man appeared after his sentence to be obdurate, and insensible of his awful situation; but afterwards, through the consolatory admonitions of the worthy clergyman, the Ordinary of the Castle, he became resigned to his unhappy fate, and died penitently.'

Booth met his fate on Monday 13th March 1820 - his body being 'dissected and anatomised.'

It is interesting to note that the hangman who hanged Booth had himself been sentenced to death twice. William Curry, whose nickname was Mutton Curry due to the type of crimes he had committed, was convicted of sheep stealing and had his sentence each time changed to transportation. In York, the holder of the hangman's post was usually a convicted villain under the sentence of death, who was pardoned on condition he accepted the unsavoury job. William Curry was in York Castle awaiting transportation to Australia when the post became vacant. Curry didn't need much persuading to accept it. A new 'drop' or gallows had been installed about the time of Curry's appointment in 1802 and over the next 33 years Curry was to preside over several dozen hangings including 14 who were all hung in one day in 1813. Curry frequently overindulged in drink leading to him bungling many hangings, which in turn meant an even worse death for his victims. Let us hope that Samuel Booth's journey into eternity was on one of Curry's better days.

Hangings were held in public until 1868

The Parkins were in the employment of the Wortley family from 1765 to 1819. Thomas of Finkle Street, Wortley was buried at St Leonard's Church Wortley on October 13th 1819 aged 31 years according to the burial register. Ages at this time are unreliable and it is possible that Thomas was the son of the Joseph who survived the attack. If so, he was baptised at St Leonard's 3rd October 1780.

William Garrett was probably one of the twin sons born to Joseph Garrett and his wife of Skew Hill, Grenoside. The other twin was named Joseph after his father; probably being the elder of the two and their baptism on the 9th Aug 1801 is recorded in the parish register of St Mary's Ecclesfield.

John and Benjamin Bower were probably the sons of Thomas Bower of Grenoside, John baptised at St Mary's Ecclesfield 26 Dec 1796 and Benjamin born Nov 7th and baptised also at St Mary's on 30th Nov 1800.

Samuel Booth I have been unable to identify as having been a Grenoside born man though there is a Samuel son of Benjamin Booth of Chapeltown who was baptised 22nd Jan 1775, making him quite a bit older than the others. As the Mercury reports that Mr Wortley 'made the most earnest intercession for the *three younger*' then it is quite probable this is the correct Samuel Booth.

Sources

Parish Records of St Mary's, Ecclesfield – Sheffield City Archives.

Sheffield Mercury, 1820 – Newspaper collection of Sheffield Local Studies Library.

Thomas Winder, ed., *An Old Ecclesfield Diary* (1921).

8. Emanuel Eaton – "The Fairyland Poet"   *Estelle Barton*

A casual visitor to Grenoside and its surrounding area might be forgiven for thinking that this has always been a quiet rural location which, until the building of the new council estates at Foxhill in the 1960s, was isolated from the noise and industry of the city of Sheffield. However, during Victorian times, the villages and hamlets of Grenoside and neighbouring areas were home to many small cottage industries. These produced handmade nails and files or made tips for shuttles, with many local farmers also doing a little metalwork to add to their income. The area would not have been such a rural idyll after all, but a place of noise and hard work, with its fair share of larger than life characters, all set against a backdrop of ancient fields and woodlands.

One such local character was Emanuel Eaton, who lived from around 1791 to 1875 and was, to quote from his tombstone in Ecclesfield churchyard, "Late of Fairyland, The Well-Known Poet and Musician". This was a man who apparently made sufficient money from working in the metal industry to retire from work at the age of fifty, buy his house and devote himself to writing poetry and music, which he performed to entertain his friends and the more well-to-do residents of the neighbourhood and their visitors. A lover of nature, gardening and, it must be said, the fairer sex, he was an eccentric who tied verses to his flowers, buried money in the garden and kept his coffin ready for use under his bed. This chapter is an attempt to bring back to life this extraordinary man and his poetry, by collecting together information gleaned from the archives of the Grenoside and District Local History Group and other sources.

The first reference to Emanuel Eaton was found in Albert Goddard's "Yesterday in Grenoside" which was written in the 1940s and recently edited and published by Chris Morley:

> A footpath across the fields brings us to Woodend. In the middle field three stone steps over the wall lead into a small plantation and the Colley Well. This was said to contain water of great medicinal value. An old resident of Woodend aptly named it "Fairyland the Blessed". There are only ten houses in this snug little nest, and there is no through thorough-fare for horse-drawn traffic, an old cartway from Feoffee's Farm being the way to and from Whitley Lane. Peggy Lane, opposite Middleton Green Fields footpath, and two bridle paths from Penistone Road through the wood are the only ways in. A Fairyland come true for anyone with imagination, a love of music and poetry, the simple natural life with no discordant notes. Birds, butterflies and flowers by day, and the delightful "little folk" as company at night. Mr. Emmanuel Eaton was a lover of music and poetry, an ardent student of nature, with a vivid imagination. A little croft at the back of his home joined up to the wood, under the overhanging branches was a stretch of short, velvety grass, sloping up from this was a grassy mound shaped like an inverted saucer with a young perfectly shaped tree at the top; a fine specimen of a sycamore – it is still there. And under this old Manny sat on warm summer nights, playing music on his violin and reciting poetry, both of his own composition, to the "little Folk" as they danced on the green carpet below. Here in the quiet solitude he composed music and poetry on the wonderful beauty and companionship of Nature. I have never seen a fairy, but if I believed that nothing existed without me having seen it, should I be wise or foolish? Mr. Eaton had his coffin made some years before he died, using it for a cupboard.

Intrigued by this description, a search of the Group's archives yielded a volume of poems by Emanuel Eaton which was published in 1867, complete with a characteristically quirky preface by the man himself and two proudly reproduced testimonials from Edinburgh and London.

A

COLLECTION

OF

ORIGINAL POEMS,.

BY E. EATON

THE FAIRYLAND POET,

FUSCHIA COTTAGE,

PALMERSTON PLACE,

NEAR GRENOSIDE.

PRINTED FOR THE AUTHOR:
JULY, 1867.

PREFACE.

FOR 24 years the late John Rodgers, Esq., of Hillsboro' Hall, and scores of others have asked me to publish my poems, but I never intended them for print, so, I hope, my readers will consider the case well, and not take it that I am stepping out in a boasting manner. If I had ever thought of printing I should not have suffered any one to copy, and I certainly should have aimed at more various themes and measures. The reason I have wrote is, I have a big fruit garden and greenhouse, so with my fiddle, flowers, fruit, funny tales, sing song and witty remarks, draws a great number of visitors, and among them the most respectable, who bring their company to be amused, as my poems express, scores of lovely ladies and bonny lassies, with their lovers, and a few old maids looking out for something bad to find. My schooling ceased in my eighth year. At sixteen I commenced making love songs; at fifty I gave up work, having made pretty fair acquaintance with yellow boys and bought my present place of residence. The old folks then living said they use to see fairies dance, and there is a lane close by called "Fairy Lane" to this day. Poet like, I claimed the title for my place. From custom it has now become appellative to me as well as my place, causing me to have a curious dream, which I have written. You must not view my poems as a criterion of my talent; if you want to see me in the true light of my capacity fix me in a suitable company, and there you will find me kindling up into lovely flame, lovely ladies, and bonny lasses. I am now in my 77th year, and am enjoying the fruits of my industry with pen, fiddle, flowers, and garden spade, and I feel as strong and active as ever, with my mind improving, Palmerston like. I expect my little bantum will have to go through the chatter house, but we are prepared for that lot, only face us fair and they will find the schoolmaster at home.

> So ladies and bonny lassies I'll relate,
> I will unto you my book dedicate.

Old Scot, the alabaster monument in Ecclesfield Church is my sleeping partner in the muses.

> Those testimonials truly tell
> That my works are original;
> They're my (Trade mark) my book denote
> Them stamp'd on every piece I've wrote.

                    EMANUEL   EATON.

TESTIMONIALS.

DEAR SIR,—I have been very much amused by the perusal of your Book of Poems, which I now beg to return. The reason of my keeping them so long was I wished to give them another perusal, as they brought to mind my favourite BURNS. I have seen many of Burns's Letters; he wrote a fine bold hand, and yours comes the nearest to it I have ever seen; I don't think any one could tell the difference. And you have Burns's genius too, which I shall be very glad to express to you personally when I see you.

To E. Eaton.   J. SELTON, Edinburgh.

                              London, 9th April, 1858.

DEAR SIR,—Many thanks for your kindness in lending me your Book of Poems, which I now beg to return. In reply to your question,—"What would the London folks say of the Fairyland Poet?" I think that I may answer that they would without doubt say that he was a thorough original. For my own part I can assure you that my recent visit to Fairyland was far from being an unprofitable one—I was not only amused, but interested. It is not every day that one meets with a character like you—a rough diamond, equally free from the cutter as the setter's craft. While I looked at and listened to you, I could not help remarking that I then enjoyed the rare privilege of studying a Poet fresh from Nature's mould—"untouched" by the hand of man.

Hoping that you may long live to *enjoy yourself* and amuse your visitors, I remain, dear Sir, very faithfully yours,

To Mr. Eaton.   GEORGE HARVEY.

The fame of this local poet was clearly slow to fade, because a cutting from a local newspaper on 22nd December 1934 devotes several inches to a description of his life and character.

A GRENOSIDE POET

VILLAGE GENIUS OF EIGHTY YEARS AGO

Dec 22. ———— 1934

A ROUGH DIAMOND

Many "mute inglorious Miltons" there may be, as Gray suggests, whose dust is intermingled with the churchyard mould; but when a rare creative spirit, having lived long and well, has demonstrated supremely intellectual powers, has won the excited admiration of his co-temporaries, and has left behind a volume of poems in which he gives to the world his choicest thoughts in his choicest language, how cruel that his memory should be allowed to fade!

Such a man "The Fairyland Poet" must have been. Did you never hear of him? Never hear of Emanuel Eaton, of Fuschia Cottage, Palmerston Place, Grenoside?

"The Fairyland Poet" lived in the pretty little hamlet of Wood End, and was in his 77th year (in 1867) when his "Collection of Original Poems" was published. He was a lover of nature, and undoubtedly possessed a markedly amorous disposition. There was fun in the earth in those days. He had a big fruit garden and a greenhouse, and by means of his fiddle, flowers, fruit, funny tales, songs, wit, and versification, he became attractive as a magnet to the people of the surrounding neighbourhood. Whitley Hall took great notice of him. He wrote at that time: "Among my numerous visitors, some are most respectable, and they bring their company to be amused. Scores of lovely ladies, bonny lassies with their lovers, and a few old maids, come to see me. You must not view my poems as a criterion of my talent—if you want to see me in the true light of my capacity, fix me in a suitable company, and then you will find me kindling up into lovely flame."

GRENOSIDE GREEN

His company was courted and his words were sought, for did he not, like a true poet, possess "the vision and the faculty divine"? Certainly he wrote from the heart, and the heart always understood him.

Here is a bit of lovely meditation from "My dream":—

"All solemn still the moon shone bright,
  The sun sank in the west,
Each twinkling star gave extra light,
  All nature's gone to rest;
That night my fiddle sounded sweet,
  But mark what did transpire,
It was my muse I had to meet,
  My fancy she did fire."

Again, how warmly he could respond to a request! Dr. Sewell, a musician of Rotherham, offered himself as a subject, with this result:—

"Dr. Sewell played well his part,
  He split my thoughts asunder,
Every note struck my fond heart,
  I count him a great wonder."

And what intense admiration the poet had for his village, e.g.:—

Oh! have you been where I have been,
Or have you seen what I have seen,
  At Grenoside, upon the green?
That is the place,
That does at morning, noon, or e'en,
  The village grace."

NO PARISH POET

The poet's muse was not restricted to narrow limits. He could write on any topic under the sun, and among the selected subjects contained in his book are:—A drowned sweetheart, Lady Milton, Whitley Hall, Warts, Porter Street, Birley House, Botanical Gardens, Lovely Ann, The Barmaid, Paddy's Pig, Blazing Comets, Pogmoor Tom, Owlerton Drummers, and King Solomon.

Occasionally Fairyland was styled Gretna Green, for one of the poet's favourite pastimes was to conduct mop weddings, and scores of young men and maidens submitted to these amusing mock-marriages.

"Such a wedding ne'er was seen,
  Fairyland held them the mop,
  While they both did over pop."

A ROUGH DIAMOND

Lest any impetuous critic should rush in and ask, "Is this poetry?" we hasten to assure him that The Fairyland Poet had behind him the backing and authority of both the English and Scottish capitals. In the foreword of the book of poems, Mr. G. Harvey, of London, writes: "It is not every day that one meets with a character like you—a rough diamond, equally free from the cutter as the setter's craft. I enjoyed the rare privilege of studying a poet fresh from nature's mould. And Mr. J. Selton, of Edinburgh, adds: "Your poems bring to mind my favourite Burns, and you have Burns' genius too."

Was the Grenoside poet eccentric? Of course he was—all men of genius are. One of his weaknesses was to tie a verse of poetry on every plant in his greenhouse. Then again, like old Shylock, he was miserly and knew how to gather in the shekels, e.g.: "At 50 I gave up work, having made pretty fair acquaintance with yellow-boys (sovereigns) and bought my place of residence." He buried his treasure in secret spots of his garden, and after his departure, six sovereigns were dug up underneath a gooseberry tree. His coffin was made to order long before his death, and was kept in readiness under his bed. In due time it had to be occupied and The Fairyland Poet was the first to be buried in the new section of the Ecclesfield churchyard.

Another mention of Emanuel Eaton was found in the Reverend J. Eastwood's "History of the Parish of Ecclesfield" published in 1879:

Whitley Carr is a detached portion of this hamlet, situated close under Greno Wood. Here is a small farmhouse belonging to the Duke of Norfolk, over the door of which is the date 1679, and initials W.W.S.; S.R. Near it resides an eccentric character, who having realized an independence by his own exertions, has retired to this sheltered nook to pass the remainder of his days, far from the sound of the tilt-hammers amid which his younger days were spent. Emmanuel Eaton, such is the worthy's name, occupies himself with cultivating choice flowers, fiddling and writing verses, the latter, if not quite (as he thinks) in the style of Burns, except in one, and that not the most creditable point of resemblance, are still curious emanations from such a source.

Some further research has revealed that Emanuel Eaton was baptised on 3rd April 1791 in Ecclesfield parish church. By the time of the 1851 census he was 60 years old, married to Sarah (aged 48) and gave his occupation as "Landed Proprietor". Also living with them was their grandson Joseph Eaton, aged 3 years. In her diary in 1856, Juliana Gatty (daughter of the Reverend Alfred Gatty who was vicar of Ecclesfield from 1839 to 1903) wrote that on 22nd March, along with two of her sisters and a brother, she went to "Emmanuel Heaton's to get some verbenas for the garden". In the 1871 census Emanuel and Sarah were living alone at Wood End, Whitley and Emanuel gave his occupation as "Retired Steel Forger". Emanuel died on 16th September 1875, aged 85 years and Sarah died 8 years later on 19th March 1883, aged 79 years.

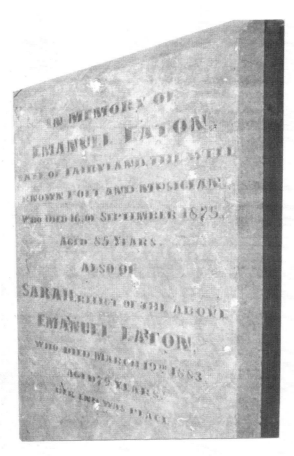

Emanuel and Sarah Eaton are buried in the graveyard of St. Mary's Church, Ecclesfield, where their gravestone can still be seen.

Emanuel Eaton's poetry is of a fairly simple sing-song style covering a range of subjects, from the beauties of nature and gardening to the admiration of young ladies. In some the tone is comic, while other poems are sincere tributes to friends and happy occasions fondly remembered. Often the poet refers to himself, as well as his home, as "Fairyland". Let the following selection of poems from the 1867 volume speak for itself, the words in square brackets are the poet's own.

WHITLY HALL

[A German gentleman asked me to compose a poem on the beautiful residence of Doctor Bingley, Whitly Hall.]

There is a bonny purling silver stream,
In a delightful little flowery glen;
Up to the wishes of a poet's dream,
A lovely subject for a poet's pen.
At eventide, when Phoebus bids adieu,
Then Whitly Hall is a delightful scene –
A settled charm one may with pleasure view,
Its bonny slopes adorn'd with verdure green.
How stately grow the lofty walnut trees,
Adding great beauty – all majestic seem,
The little warblers tuning all to peace,
And fishes playing in the silver stream.
Beauties of Nature largely has combin'd,
To decorate this lovely rural manse;

It leaves all other mansions far behind,
Its situation's so far in advance.
On its bonny banks the fair primroses grow,
Where't merry youngsters pass the merry hours;
In the neat garden the moss-roses blow,
Mixing their fragrance with sweet beds of flowers.
The smooth glossy lake is not without fish,
Which nightly strollers are so well aware;
And fairplay anglers have oft filled their dish,
And poachers come in for their ill-earned share.
The parents love to see their children play,
In their fine garden among the flowers gay:
In happiness may all go hand in hand,
And not forgetting funny Fairyland.

PORTER STREET

In Master Woodcock I delight,
An able commentator;
With ready wit a genius bright,
A model form'd by nature.

He'll step out o'er and o'er again,
A critic very able;
With minuteness he will explain,
To all around the table.

We listened with cheerfulness,
Unto his nice discerning;
So what he is I'll have a guess,
A Philo fond of learning.

And Mr. Deakin goes well through,
His acts in gallant style O;
He's got a gift of Nature's gift,
No doubt another Philo.

I ne'er had such a happy night,
As at this music meeting;

Ladies more like angels bright,
With gracefulness complete in.

To me was great attention paid,
To all good things invited;
Bountiful was the table spread;
In my songs they delighted.

Young ladies to 't piano sung,
With such sweet lovely graces;
With their sweet voices the room rung,
Caus'd many smiling faces.

Doctor Sewel played well his part,
He split my thoughts assunder;
Every note struck my fond heart,
I count him a great wonder.

The whole night through was joy and mirth,
In my soul 'twas engraven;
It's really heaven upon earth,
New Porter-street, number eleven.

MISS CRESWICK, DRESSMAKER

We have autumn now in view,
And the swallow bid adieu,
Sweet Robin is chirping at my door;
And chilly is the breeze,
Blowing through the naked trees,
The beauty of my greenhouse is no more.

There's something left behind,
Very cheering to my mind,
My fiddle which I do highly prize;
With its never failing cheers,
To me and the lovely dears,
With their very charming bonny bright eyes.

But Miss Creswick takes the lead,
With her needle and her thread,
And all things she takes in hand:

Quickly makes her scissors cut,
Though they neither ope nor shut,
Surpassing all e'er came to Fairyland.

In her very pretty face,
There's abundance of sweet grace,
Her bonny black eyes do declare:
Pleasing manners and much wit,
Makes her every way complete,
With her neatly put up raven locky hair.

Her fond parents do delight,
In their loving favourite,
Virtue's path she has paid much regard:
With such a virtuous mind,
A noble pattern for her kind,
Future happiness await her just reward.

ORDER TO HANDSWORTH

Fourteen plants in the bill I find,
But thirteen in the hamper spy;
So there's a fuchsia left behind,
That is the bonnie butterfly.

You have not sent the butterfly;
Please say why it did not take wing?
And please tell Master Tingle why
The butterfly was not put in?

It does appear, somehow or other,
A slight mistake there has been,
The hamper would not hold another
When you had put in the thirteen.

To me it is a pitiful case
That it has so omitted been;

Please send it to make up my place,
To make a complete fairy scene.

Attention to it shall be paid,
I will keep it both neat and clean,
Butterfly shall be lady's maid
Unto my lovely Fairy Queen.

They shall be fixed side by side
The lovely ladies' smile to court,
Flora herself will take pride
To view scenes lovely of this sort;

Cuckoo will o'er my greenhouse cry
"Cuckoo!" nine times ev'ry hour,
Peeping at my bonnie butterfly,
With its delightful tip'd flower.

LOST THEIR PEARS

Two smart young bucks from Grenoside
Came linking with their lovely dears,
At a pleasant time, sweet eventime,
To taste my apples and my pears.

The lasses half-way in their teens,
Both were trimmed off so very gay,
Two bonnie bashful virgin queens,
Just from their mammies stole away.

Miss M. had a red rosey face,
A very bonnie brisk young maid,
Adorned with sweet lovely grace –
A pity beauty e'er should fade.

Miss Lucy was drest very neat,
A very Venus seemed to be,
Her fairy form was so complete,
The prettiest girl I e'er did see.

Tom said "My apples were not good,
So bring some pears for our misses."
Perhaps as they came down the wood
They'd been exchanging honey kisses.

The ripest apple ever grown,
Nor yet the sweetest mellow pear
Is half so sweet plain truth will own
As a kiss from a Lucy dear.

Next morning up to the wood I went,
I stood a little looking round,
The lovely dears had lost their pears,
They all lay scattered on the ground.

But how it was we may suppose,
But hope the journey ended well;
They surely nothing else did lose,
But coming cuckoo time will tell.

Sources

Census records for Grenoside, 1851 and 1871.

Revd. J. Eastwood, *A History of the Parish of Ecclesfield* (London, 1879).

E. Eaton, *A Collection of Original Poems* (1867).

Fulleylove Collection of Newspaper Cuttings – Grenoside & District Local History Group Archives.

Albert Goddard, *Yesterday in Grenoside* (2000).

Joan and Mel Jones, *The Remarkable Gatty Family of Ecclesfield* (Green Tree Publications, Thorpe Hesley, 2003).

Parish Records of St Mary's, Ecclesfield – Sheffield City Archives.

9. Sparrow Pie: Life in Service at Birley Hall in the 1930s

Elsie Taylor   (selected by Graham Slater)

Birley House - sometimes known as Birley Hall.

BREAKFAST - for the better classes consisted of porridge, bacon, eggs, sausages, kidneys or haddock or kippers, kedgeree or fishcakes. Working class families in those days never ate fish for breakfast and thought it quite abnormal for anyone else to do so. Sometimes cold ham and boiled eggs graced the sideboard, for family and friends in those days helped themselves to the breakfast dish of their choice when they arrived down stairs for breakfast. This proved to be a leisurely meal, much to the annoyance of the servants who were anxious to get on with the chores for the day, and did not want interruption from the dining room to replenish such things as hot water for further coffee making. Coffee was the morning beverage, taken in large cups which held about 3/4 pint and was made in a 'Cona coffee machine' from freshly made coffee. This was done by means of a spirit lamp, hence the request for almost boiling water from the kitchen.

LUNCH - This was usually a two course meal, but plentiful by today's standards as a main meal. There was always a roast or meat dish which varied day by day according to the mistresses request, followed by a sweet dish also of her choosing, after a discussion with the cook prompt at nine o'clock.

AFTERNOON TEA - This was served in the drawing room and was quite a cosy, elegant little light entertainment of the day, and was also the time when family and friends gathered together for an hour to sip tea, made again from a spirit kettle of beautiful silver previously filled with boiling water from the kitchen and elegantly presided over by the lady of the house. The tea was taken in beautiful china cups, and an assortment of cakes, very thin bread and butter, hot buttered scones and crumpets were served in lovely dishes with covers to keep them hot.

DINNER - On the first stroke of seven the master would strike the gong and the soup or whatever the first course might be was expected to be entering the dining room and be placed on the table by the time the clock had finished chiming. Small wonder that there was panic stations now and again on the other side of the "green baize door". Why a "green baize door"? Kitchen smells did not penetrate into the better quarter by always keeping that door closed except for passing through it. The rest of the meal followed, course by course, as per announcement - fish, entrees, pheasant, partridge, pigeon, woodcock, hare, venison, in fact all things that I had seldom seen let alone prepared, cooked or eaten.

Wild duck - I loathed it being so difficult to pluck, but when the family had been shooting, sooner or later the spoils appeared in the kitchen to be dealt with.

I had a few embarrassing moments in my time. One occasion always comes to mind. The sons of the house had decided to clean out the trout pool and brought into the kitchen a bath full of small trout. "How in heaven's name to kill that lot and prepare it?". In the end I asked my mistress if she knew. "Take them out of the water and cook them as you would whitebait" she said. Thus armed with chip pans I began to separate fish from the water then to gather up those, that got away, from the kitchen floor. It is quite comical now that I look back but at the time I wished those sons and their whitebait anywhere but my kitchen.

The next worst thing was the sparrows! These were destroying the property by building their nests where they were not welcome, so a day's shooting took place with air guns and the poor little birds brought for me to prepare and cook. Forty-four of them in all. I think that today's young women would go on strike rather than face that lot, but such had been our training that we blindly obeyed and did our best, which was expected of us. Hence my first 'sparrow pie' was baked and I think that it was my only one - I never remember another one being baked.

Venison, when we had it, was purchased from the Earl of Wharncliffe. When a stag was killed only one haunch was required at Wortley Hall, so I was sent along with two corgies to walk from Birley Hall which is at the top of the hill known as Birley Edge, which now overlooks Batchelors canning factory to Wharncliffe Chase, a distance of I should think 4-5 miles each way and with a haunch of venison to carry on the way back. This was purchased for 4p a pound. It was wrapped in a flour and water paste to cook it, as kitchen foil was unheard of, but this kept all the succulent juices inside and prevented the meat from drying out. This was served with redcurrant jelly made from the kitchen garden fruit (as were the jams and jellies).

This reminds me of hours of helping during the afternoon to gather strawberries, raspberries, currants and gooseberries in their season, and whatever else had been grown by the gardeners. We would then sort out the choicest for serving as dessert, which meant more beautiful china plates, silver pearl handled cutlery and exquisite finger bowls being added to the rest of the fine tableware used.

Hams and pork were purchased from my parents who kept pigs at their little cottage (Little Intake) in the woods about two miles from where I worked. My father delivered the pork meat whenever he killed a pig (thereby hangs another tale). The loins were cooked as a joint, one whole loin of twelve chop size being cooked at a time, usually for Saturday lunch. The hams were taken into the cellars and placed on a stone slab, rubbed well with brown West India sugar, till the rind began to sweat, then sprinkled with saltpetre which was again rubbed into the meat, especially around the knuckle bone, then the whole legs were thickly covered with crushed dry salt and left for about 3-4 weeks. They were then brought up from the cellar, thoroughly washed and wiped dry then hung on the ceiling by 'S' hooks. These were fixed into a piece of the skin at the base of the leg, to hooks which were permanently screwed into the ceiling joists for this purpose. My father enjoyed these days as he was liberally supplied with whisky whilst he worked!

Another thing we used to do was to make cherry brandy from the morello cherries grown on a tree on one of the garden walls - also damson gin. This was done by piercing each piece of fruit several times with a large needle, putting the fruit into preserving jars, adding chopped sugar candy and covering all that with good quality brandy or gin. This was then kept for six months, when the syrupy spirit which was now a liqueur was bottled. The fruit which remained was coated with icing and served as a dessert. I have never tasted any of these since those days.

The gentry, of course, drank all kinds of wines and champagne, but they took good care of their servants and we always ate very well. It was mostly the same food, of course, after it had been into the dining room but I certainly cooked and ate dishes in those days that it would be impossible to afford now, but meat was then plentiful and of good quality and inferior cuts were cheap and affordable by the working classes. I think that only during the strikes of 1926 until the rationing of world war two were we really hungry.

The rationing was a poor time but then again if like us you lived in the country you were allowed to keep a pig but you had to forfeit the bacon ration for at least two members of the family. Also of course pig feeding meant hard work, collecting scraps of which there were few, small potatoes, nettles, dandelion - anything that helped the small supply of meal allowed. It was marvellous however to give family and friends a meal of bacon or ham or when the pigs were slaughtered, pork pies, brawn, sausages, pigs fry, it certainly seemed worth all the nine months of struggling. The village midwife always called for her fry and lard, bless her, and we tried to show our appreciation to our doctor as they were very hard pressed people at that time. However life was lived, not passed through, and food was something to be earned and be thankful for and shared and enjoyed. It made our social life as friends and relatives came to a meal and were given the best that we had, and they stayed talking and singing ballads and telling jokes, these indeed were days to remember.

Biographical Notes on the Authors and Contributors

Philip Allison

Philip was born in 1913 in Nether Edge. His family moved to Penistone but returned to Sheffield in 1923. Originally educated at Hunter's Bar School, he gained a scholarship to Greystones Intermediate. After two years at Central Secondary School he won a technical studentship to Sheffield University where he emerged, four years later, with a First Class Honours Degree in Civil Engineering, in 1934.

After working in Middlesborough and in Sheffield for 8 months, he went south to London to work for a civil engineering consultant. After a year he returned briefly to Sheffield to marry his long-time sweetheart, Mary, and they lived happily in Hampstead until the outbreak of World War Two. Having been evacuated from London, the Allisons moved eleven times over five years to places including Surrey, Chepstow, Newport, Monmouthshire and Farnborough, as wartime projects came and went.

When the war was over Philip continued as a civil engineer for the Royal Aircraft Establishment, Farnborough, Hampshire, until 1949 when a job cropped up in the City Engineer's Department in Sheffield. And so Philip and Mary returned to their home town to live at Nether Edge. In 1986 they moved to Grenoside, their 17th house, where they still reside.

Philip has many interests including painting and Probus Club, but it is his involvement in the Local History Group from which his choice of subject here arises. It is partly inherited from his father's interest in, and writing about, the early crucible steel industry.

Estelle Barton

Estelle was born and raised in Buxton, Derbyshire and from there went on to gain a university education. Until recently she pursued a career as a research fellow in the field of cancer epidemiology, working for many years at the University of Birmingham, before returning north to take up a post at Leeds University in 1998. Shortly after this, in 1999, she moved to Grenoside with her husband Jeff who was originally from the nearby Foxhill neighbourhood of Sheffield. Estelle now works part time at the Royal Hallamshire Hospital, Sheffield as an academic secretary, helping with the setting up and running of clinical trials in the clinical research unit of the Haematology department.

Having taken an old house in the very heart of Grenoside village Estelle was naturally interested in its history, and working part time enabled her to join the thriving Grenoside and District Local History Group. Browsing through the Group's library and archives has given her fascinating glimpses of people and events from the area's past, including one local eccentric, the poet Emanuel Eaton.

David Diver

David was born, lived and worked in London until retirement prompted him to move from that over-crowded and uncaring city to a viilage where people actually said "Good morning" in the street even to a newcomer they didn't know. He spent his working life as a buyer in a series of industrial companies, ending as a Contracts Manager with British Gas. He now lives in Grenoside with his wife Thelma and Jack – a border collie of great friendliness and limited intelligence.

His interest in gannister arises from his involvement in purchasing raw materials for a company which manufactured various carbon materials such as electrical brushes and crucibles. A visit to a graphite mine in Germany sparked a fascination for the way minerals are extracted from the Earth. It came as a complete surprise to find that within a mile of his new address is a maze of tunnels laboriously dug into the hillside from which, for nearly a hundred years, a rock – vital to the steel industry – was extracted.

Nev Hayward

Nev(ille) was educated at Gravesend Technical College and served a general engineering apprenticeship before joining the Royal Air Force to undertake his two years of National Service. After this, he married and settled in Waltham Cross, employed as a draughtsman. In 1976 the company he was working for moved to Chapeltown – he came north with it. His leisure time has been filled by numerous interests which included learning something of his new surroundings. Upon retirement in 1996 he joined a Local History Study Group which was part of Sheffield College. When this disbanded he joined the Grenoside and District Local History Group to further this interest.

During a walk along nearby Wharncliffe Crags Nev was told that 2000 years ago the area was the site of a Romano-British quern factory. Anxious to find out more he delved into the Group's archives and Sheffield's City Library for more information. The results are set out in his chapter on Querns.

Lyn Howsam

Lyn is a Sheffielder by birth and has lived in the north of the city all her life. She attended the City Grammar School and after marrying Alan and having her two sons went to work for the NHS spending twenty years at the Northern General Hospital. She became very interested in the history of the hospital that had started out life as the Fir Vale Workhouse and recently had a book published entitled 'Memories of the Workhouse & Old Hospital at Fir Vale'. She has been a member of the Grenoside & District Local History Group for over two years now. Over the years Lyn has had a wide range of interests but her main ones now are genealogy, local history, writing and gardening. While tracing her family history and finding some quite interesting characters along the way she came across a copy of 'An Old Ecclesfield Diary' in her local library. An entry in it for 1790 led to her discovering that her four times great grandmother had been killed by a bear. Another intriguing entry that caught Lyn's eye was about Samuel Booth, a Grenoside man who was hanged at York. When she joined our group it was one of the things she decided to research into. Her interest in nailmaking stems yet again from her family history as one of her possible ancestors is Jonathan Deardon, Nail Chapman, who was one of the main men responsible for the drawing up of the Nailmakers Agreement in 1733.

Graham Slater

Graham was born in Grenoside in the early 1930s, at the corner of Bower Lane and Cupola, in a little cottage which, sadly, no longer exists.

His family moved to Sheffield when he was ten. After starting his career as a technician at Sheffield University, he transferred to Imperial College in London where he spent fourteen years before homesickness brought him back north in the mid 1970s. He became Granville College's Principal Technician until retirement five years ago.

He now lives at Dronfield, but his roots remain firmly planted in Grenoside. This feeling of belonging to the village prompted him to join the Local History Group to try and fill in his knowledge of his family's association with the area.

Since joining the Group he has helped with the archives and is the main user of our computer. Keenly interested in his own family history he is anxious to encourage others to find out and record their own family's life for the interest and benefit of future generations.

He has chosen an extract from our archives written by Elsie Taylor who, despite her considerable age, can still paint a vigorous picture of what life in service was like in the 1930s.

Sam Sykes

Born in 1953, Sam's education culminated in an Honorary Arts Degree and a Masters Degree in Local History. Thus armed he negotiated on behalf of the National Union of Mineworkers and followed this by involvement with the re-education of the army of redundant steelworkers. This led to his involvement in Adult Education with Sheffield City Council. It was at this time that he became involved with the Local History Groups at Chapeltown and Grenoside. When Sheffield decided it could no longer afford such extravagances as Adult Education it was Sam's enthusiastic encouragement which led to the formation of the present Grenoside and District Local History Group. After a period with Age Concern at Bradford, Sam is back in Sheffield again, working as Sector Manager for Private Sector Renewal. Any spare time he has is swallowed up by his smallholding, reflecting his interest in and love of our environment and heritage.

Elsie Taylor

Elsie Taylor (nee Wragg) was born almost 88 years ago. She was a major contributor to one of our earlier publications, "Memories of Grenoside", and the short extract which Graham Slater has selected from our archives is both an example of her vigorous style and a reminder of a way of life that hardly exists today. Elsie grew up on a small farmstead in the middle of Wharncliffe Woods. She attended Barnsley Girl's High School and at the age of 16 took up the post of housemaid at Birley Hall. In later years Elsie and her husband lived in Watford, but eventually they returned to Grenoside, living for a time at the top of St. Helena (Holly House Lane). At present Elsie is busy writing a full account of her life. We look forward to it.

Grenoside & District Local History Group
www.grenosidelocalhistory.co.uk

The Grenoside & District Local History Group was formed in 1997 having earlier started life as a local education class. Membership is open to anyone with an interest in Grenoside and its surrounding area. The Group aims are to hold events, collect material and publish information to stimulate the interest and knowledge of Grenoside.

We encourage and support individuals in their own research as well as developing group research. As a group we are also interested in hearing from people who no longer live in the area but have memories, memorabilia and photos of the area which they would be willing to share with us.

Our meetings range from workshops, and informal meetings to visiting speakers, who cover a wide rage of local and family history subjects. We also have a monthly visit to a place of historical interest; duration of approximately 3-6 hours.

We meet every Tuesday at 10am - 12 noon, between September and July, with the exception of school holidays, in the Lower Hall of Grenoside Community Centre, Main Street, Grenoside. Visitors are always welcome.

For further information visit our website, or telephone our Secretary, Estelle Barton, on 0114 257 1929.

Members of the Group on a visit to Conisbrough Castle.